Mayne Reid

The Free Lance

A Romance of the Mexican Valley. Vol. 1

Mayne Reid

The Free Lance
A Romance of the Mexican Valley. Vol. 1

ISBN/EAN: 9783744673785

Printed in Europe, USA, Canada, Australia, Japan

Cover: Foto ©Thomas Meinert / pixelio.de

More available books at **www.hansebooks.com**

A ROMANCE OF THE MEXICAN VALLEY.

BY

CAPTAIN MAYNE REID.

IN THREE VOLUMES.

VOL. I.

LONDON:

REMINGTON & CO.,

134 NEW BOND STREET.

1881.

CONTENTS.

THE FREE LANCES.

CHAPTER I.

VOLUNTEERS FOR TEXAS.

"I'LL go!"

This laconism came from the lips of a young man who was walking along the Levee of New Orleans. Just before giving utterance to it he had made a sudden stop, facing a dead wall, enlivened,

1

however, by a larger poster, on which were printed, in conspicuous letters, the words—

"VOLUNTEERS FOR TEXAS!"

Underneath, in smaller type, was a proclamation setting forth the treachery of Sānta Anna and the whole Mexican nation, recalling in strong terms the massacre of Fanning, the butchery of Alamo, and other like atrocities; ending in an appeal to all patriots and lovers of freedom to arm, take the field, and fight against the tyrant of Mexico and his myrmidons.

"I'll go!" said the young man, after a glance given to the printed statement; then, more deliberately re-reading them, he repeated the words with an emphasis that told of his being in earnest.

The poster also gave intimation of a meeting to be held the same evening at a certain *rendezvous* in Poydras Street.

He who read only lingered to make note of

the address, which was the name of a noted *café*. Having done this, he was turning to continue his walk when his path was barred by a specimen of humanity, who stood full six foot six in a pair of alligator leather boots, on the *banquette* by his side.

"So ye're goin', air ye?" was the half interrogative speech that proceeded from the individual thus confronting him.

"What's that to you?" bluntly demanded the young fellow, his temper a little ruffled by what appeared an impertinent obstruction on the part of some swaggering bully.

"More'n you may think for, young 'un," answered the booted Colossus, still standing square in the way; "more'n you may think for, seein' it's through me that bit o' paper's been put up on that ere wall."

"You're a bill-sticker, I suppose?" sneeringly retorted the "young 'un".

"Ha! ha! ha!" laughed the giant, with a cachination that resembled the neighing of a horse. "A bill-sticker, eh! Wal; I likes that. An' I likes yur grit, too, young feller, for all ye are so sassy. But ye needn't git riled, an' I reckon ye won't, when I tell ye who I am."

"And who are you; pray?"

"May be ye mount a hearn o' Cris Rock?"

"What! Cris Rock of Texas? He who at Fanning's——

"At Fannin's massacree war shot dead, an' kim alive agin."

"Yes," said the interrogator, whose interrogatory referred to the almost miraculous escape of one of the betrayed victims of the Goliad butchery.

"Jess so, young feller. An' since ye 'pear to know somethin' 'bout me, I needn't tell ye I ain't no *bill-sticker*, nor why I 'peared to show impartinence by putting in my jaw when I heern ye sing out, 'I'll go'. I thort it would't need much introduxshun to one as I mout soon hope to call kumarade. Yer comin' to the rendevvoo the night, ain't ye?"

"Yes ; I intend doing so."

"Wal, I'll be there myself ; an' if ye'll only look high enough, I reck'n ye kin sight me 'mong the crowd. 'Tain't like to be the shortest thar," he added, with a smile that bespoke pride in his superior stature, " tho' ye'll see some tall uns too. Anyhow jest look out for Cris Rock ; and, when foun', that chile may be of some sarvice to ye."

" I shall do so," rejoined the other, whose good humour had become quite restored.

About to bid good-bye, Rock held out a hand, broad as the blade of a canoe-paddle. It was freely taken by the stranger, who, while shaking it, saw that he was being examined from head to foot.

"Look hyar!" pursued the Colossus, as if struck by some thought which a closer scrutiny of the young man's person had suggested; "hev ye ever did any sogerin'? Ye've got the look o'it."

"I was educated in a military school—that's all."

"Whar? In the States?"

"No. I am from the other side of the Atlantic."

"Oh! A Britisher. Wal, that don't make no difference in Texas. Thar's all sorts thar. English, ain't ye?"

"No," promptly answered the stranger, with a slight scornful curling of the lip: "I'm an Irishman, and not one of those who deny it."

"All the better for that. Thar's a bit of

the same blood somewhar in my own veins, out o' a grandmother, I b'lieve, as kim over the mountains into Kaintuck, 'long wi' Dan Boone an' his lot. So ye've been eddycated at a milintary school then? D'ye unnerstan' anything about the trainin' o' sogers?

" Certainly I do."

" Dog-goned, ef you ain't the man we want! How'd ye like to be an officer? I reck'n ye're best fit for that."

" Of course I should like it; but as a stranger among you I shouldn't stand much chance of being elected. You choose your officers, don't you?"

" Sartin, we eelect 'em; an' we're goin' to to hold the eelections this very night. Lookee hyar, young fellur; I like yer looks, an' I've seed proof ye've got the stuff in ye. Now I want to tell ye somethin' ye oughter to know. I belong to this company that's jest a formin',

and thar's a fellur settin' hisself up to be its
capting.   He's a sort o' half Spanish, half
French Creole, o' Noo-Orleans hyar, an' we
old Texans don't think much o' him.   But
thar's only a few o' us; while 'mong the Orleans
city fellurs' as are goin' out to, he's got a big
pop'larity by standin' no eend o' drinks.   He
aint a bad lookin' sort for sogerin' and hez seen
milintary sarvice, they say.   F'r all that thar'
a hang-dog glint 'bout his eyes this child don't
like; neither do some o' the others.   So young
un, if you'll come down to the rendyvoo in
good time an' make a speech—you kin speech-
ify, can't ye."

"Oh, I suppose I could say something."

"Wal, you stump it, an' I'll put in a word
or two an' then we'll perpose ye for capting;
an' who knows we mayent git the majority
arter all?   You'er willin' to try, aint ye?"

"Quite willing," answered the Irishman,

with an emphasis which showed how much the proposal was to his mind. "But why, Mr. Rock, are you not a candidate yourself? You have seen service, and would make a good officer, I should say."

"Me kandydate for officer! Wal! I'm big enough thet's true, and ef you like ugly enuf. But I aint no ambeeshum thet way. Besides this chile knows nothin' 'bout *drill;* an' thet's what's wanted bad. Ye see we aint had much reg'lar sogerin' in Texas. Thar's whar the Mexikins hev the advantage o' us an' thar's whar you'll hev the same if you'll consent to stan'. You say you will?"

"I will if you wish it."

"All square then," returned the Texan, once more taking his *protégé* by the hand, and giving it a squeeze like the grip of a grizzly bear. "I'll be on the look-out for ye. Meanwhile thar's six hours to the good yet afore it

git sundown. So go and purpar' yur speech,
while I slide roun' among the fellurs an' do a
leetle for ye in the line o' canvassin."

After a final bruin-like pressure of the
hand the giant had commenced striding away,
when he again came to a halt, uttering a loud
"Hiloo!"

"What is it?" inquired the young Irishman.

"It seems that Cris Rock air 'bout one o'
the biggest nummorskulls in all Noo-Orleans.
Only to think! I was about startin' to take
the stump for a kandydate 'ithout knowin' the
first letter o' his name. How wur ye crissened,
young fellur?"

"Kearney—Florence Kearney."

"Florence, ye say? Aint that a woman's
name?"

"True; but in Ireland many men bear
it?"

"Wal, it do seem a little kewrious; but it'll do right slick, an' the Kearney part souns well. I've hearn speak o' Kate Kearney; thar's a song 'bout the gurl. Mout ye be any connexshun o' hern?"

"No, Mr. Rock, not that I'm aware of. She was a Killarney woman. I was born a little further north on the green island."

"Wal: no matter what part o' it, yur are welkim to Texas, I reck'n, or the States eyther. Kearney—I like the name. It hev a good ring, an' it'll soun' all the better wi' 'Capting' for a handle to 't—the which it shall hev afore ten o'clock this night, if Cris Rock ain't astray in his reck'nin. But see as ye kum early to the rendyvoo, so as 't hev time for a talk wi' the boys. Thar's a somethin' in that; an' if ye've got a ten dollar bill to spare spend it on drinks all round. Thar's a good deal in that too."

So saying, the Texan strode off, leaving Florence Kearney to reflect upon the counsel so opportunely extended.

CHAPTER II.

A LADY IN THE CASE.

HO Florence Kearney was, and what his motive for becoming a "filibuster," the reader shall be told without much tediousness of detail.

Some six months before the encounter described, he had landed from a Liverpool cotton ship on the Levee of New Orleans. A gentleman by birth and a soldier-scholar by education, he had gone to the New World with the design

to complete his boyhood's training by a course
of travel, and prepare himself for the enacting
the *metier* of a man.   That this travel should
be westward, over fresh untrodden fields, instead of along the hackneyed highways of the
of the European tourist, was partly due to the
counsels of a tutor—who had himself visited
the New World—and partly to his own natural
inclinations.

In the course of his college studies he had
read the romantic history of Cortez's conquest,
and his mind had become deeply imbued with
the picturesqueness of Mexican scenes; so that
among the fancies of his youthful life one of
the pleasantest was that of some day visiting
the land of Anahuac, and its ancient capital,
Tenochtitlan.   After leaving college the dream
had grown into a determination, and was now
in the act of being realised.   In New Orleans
he was so far on his way.   He came thither

expecting to obtain passage in a coasting vessel to some Mexican seaport—Tampico or Vera Cruz.

Why he had not at once continued his journey thither was due to no diffculty in finding such a vessel. There were schooners sailing every week to either of the above ports that would have accommodated him, yet still he lingered in New Orleans. His reason for thus delaying was one far from uncommon— this being a lady with whom he had fallen in love.

At first the detention had been due to a more sensible cause. Not speaking the Spanish language, which is also that of Mexico, he knew that while travelling through the latter country he would have to go as one dumb. In New Orleans he might easily obtain a teacher; and having sought soon found one, in the person of Don Ignacio Valverde,—a refugee Mexican gentleman, a victim of the tyrant Santa Anna, who, banished from his country, had been for several years resident in the States as an exile. And an exile in straitened circumstances, one of the hardest conditions of life. Once in his own country a wealthy land owner, Don Ignacio was now compelled to give lessons in Spanish to such stray pupils as might chance to present themselves. Among the rest by chance, came Florence Kearney, to whom he had commenced teaching it.

But while the latter was making himself master of the Andalusian tongue, he also learnt to love one who spoke it as purely, and far more sweetly, than Don Ignacio. This was Don Ignacio's daughter.

* * * * * * * *

After parting with Cris Rock, the young Irishman advanced along the Levee, his head bowed forward, with eyes to the ground, as if examining the oyster shells that thickly bestrewed the path; anon giving his glance to the river, as though stirred by its majestic movement. But he was thinking neither of the empty bivalves, nor the flow of the mighty stream. Nor yet of the speech he had promised to make that same night at the rendezvous of filibusters. Instead he was reflecting upon that affair of the heart, from which he had been some time suffering.

To make known his feelings it is necessary to repeat what passed through his mind after he had separated from the Texan.

"There's something odd in all this," soliloquised he, as he strode on. "Here am I going to fight for a country I care nothing about, and against one with which I have no cause of quarrel. On the contrary, I have come four thousand miles to visit the latter, as a peaceful friendly traveller. Now I propose making

2

entry into it, sword in hand, as an enemy and invader ! The native land too of her, who has taken possession of my heart! Ah! therein lies the very reason : *I have not got her's.* I fear— nay, I am certain of that, from what I saw this morning. Bah ! What's the use of thinking about it, or about her ? Luisa Valverde cares no more for me than the half-score of others— these young Creole ' bloods,' as they call them- selves—who flit like butterflies around her. She's a sweet flower from which all of them wish to sip. Only one will succeed, and that's Carlos Santander. I hate the very sight of the man. I believe him to be a cheat and a scoundrel. No matter to her. The cheat she won't understand ; and, if report speak true of her country and race, the scoundrel would scarcely qualify him either. Merciful heavens! to think I should love this Mexican girl, warned as I've been about her country-women ! 'Tis a fascination and the sooner I get away from it, and her presence, the better it may be for me. Now, this Texan business offers a chance of escaping the peril. If I find she cares not for me, it will be a sort of satisfaction to think that in fighting against her country I may in a way humiliate herself. Ah, Texas! If you find in me a defender it will not be from any patriotic love of you but to bury bitter thoughts in oblivion."

The chain of his reflections momentarily interrupted, was after a time continued : " My word," he exclaimed, " there's surely something ominous in my encounter with this Cris Rock! Destiny seems to direct me. Here am I scheming to escape from a thraldom of a siren's smiles, and, to do so, ready to throw myself into the ranks of a filibustering band! On the instant a friend is found—a patron who promises to make me their leader! Shall I

refuse the favour, which fortune herself seems
to offer? Why should I? It is fate not
chance; and this night at their meeting I
shall know whether it is meant in earnest.
So, canvas your best for me, Cris Rock; and I
shall do my best to make a suitable speech.
If our united efforts prove successful, then
Texas shall gain a friend, and Luisa Valverde
lose *one* of her lovers."

At the conclusion of this speech—half
boastful, half bitter—Florence Kearney had
reached the hotel where he was stopping—
the celebrated " St. Charles," and entering its
grand saloon, sat down to reflect further on
the step he was about to take.

Chapter III.

OFFICERING THE FILIBUSTERS.

THE volunteer *rendezvous* was in a tavern, better known by the name of "Coffee House," in the street called Poydras. The room which had been chartered for the occasion was of ample dimensions, capable of containing three hundred men. Drawn together by the printed proclamation that had attracted the attention of the young Irishman in his afternoon stroll, two-

thirds of the above number had collected
together, and of these at least one-half were
determined upon proceeding to Texas.

It was a crowd composed of heterogeneous
elements—such as has ever been, and ever
will be, the men who volunteer for a military,
more especially a filibustering, expedition.

Present in the hall were representatives of
almost every civilised nation upon earth.
Even some that could scarce boast of civilisa-
tion; for among the faces seen around the
room were many so covered with beards, and
so browned with sun, as to tell of long sojourn
in savage parts, if not association with the
savages themselves.

In obedience to the counsels of the Texan,
Florence Kearney—a candidate for command
over this motley crew—made early appearance
in their midst. Not so early as to find that,
on entering the room, he was a stranger to its

occupants. Cris Rock had been there before him, along with a half-score of his *confreres*— old Texans of the pure breed—who having taken part in most of the struggles of the young Republic, had strayed back to New Orleans, partly for a spree, and partly to recruit fresh comrades to aid them in propagating that principle which had first taken them to Texas—the " Monroe Doctrine".

To these the young Irishman was at once confidentially introduced, and " stood drinks " freely. He would have done so without care of what was to come of it; since it was but the habit of his generous nation. Nor would this of itself have given him any great advantage, for not long after entering the room, he discovered that not only drinks, but dollars, were distributed freely by the opposition party, who seemed earnestly bent upon making a captain of their candidate.

As yet Kearney had not looked upon his competitor, and was even ignorant of his name. Soon, however, it was communicated to him, just as the man himself, escorted by a number of friends, made his appearance in the room. The surprise of the young Irishman may be imagined, when he saw before him one already known, and too well known, his rival in the affections of Luisa Valverde !

Yes ; Carlos Santander was also a candidate for the command of the filibusters.

To Kearney the thing was a surprise, and something besides. He knew Santander to be on terms of very friendly and intimate relationship not only with Don Ignacio, but other Mexicans he had met at the exile's house. Strange, that the Creole should be aspiring to the leadership of a band about to invade their country ! For it was *invasion* the Texans now talked of, in retaliation for a late raid of the

Mexicans to their capital, San Antonio. But these banished Mexicans being enemies of Santa Anna, it was after all not so unnatural. By humiliating the Dictator, they would be aiding their own party to get back into power —even though the help came from their hereditary foemen, the squatters of Texas.

All this passed through the mind of the young Irishman, though not altogether to satisfy him. The presence of Santander there as aspirant for leadership seemed strange notwithstanding.

But he had no opportunity for indulging in conjectures—only time to exchange frowns at his rival and competitor, when a man in undress uniform—a Texan colonel—who acted as chairman of the meeting, mounting upon a table, cried "Silence!" and, after a short pithy speech, proposed that the election of officers should at once proceed. The proposal was seconded, no one objecting ; and, without further parley, the " balloting " began.

There was neither noise nor confusion. Indeed, the assembly was one of the quietest, and without any street crowd outside. There were reasons for observing a certain secrecy in the proceedings ; for, although the movement was highly popular all over the States, there were some compromising points of International law, and there had been talk of Government interference.

The election was conducted in the most primitive and simple fashion. The names of the candidates were written upon slips of paper, and distributed throughout the room— only the members who had formed the organisation having the right to vote. Each of them chose the slip bearing the name of him he intended to vote for, and dropped it into a hat carried round for the purpose.

The other he threw away, or slipped into his pocket.

When all had deposited their ballots, the hat was capsized, and the bits of paper shaken out upon the table. The chairman, assisted by two other men, examined the votes and counted them. Then ensued a short interval of silence, broken only by an occasional word of direction from the chairman, with the murmuring hum of the examiners, and at length came in a clear loud voice—that of the Texan colonel—" *The votes are in favour of Kearney! Florence Kearney elected Captain by a majority of thirty-three* ".

A cheer greeted the announcement, in which something like a screech from Cris Rock could be heard above all voices ; while the giant himself was seen rushing through the crowd to clasp the hand of his *protégé*, whom he had voluntarily assisted in promoting to a rank above himself.

During the excitement, the defeated candidate was observed to skulk out of the room.
Those who saw him go could tell by his look
of sullen disappointment he had no intention
of returning ; and that the filibustering cohort
was not likely to have the name, " Carlos
Santander," any longer on its roll-call.

He and his were soon forgotten. The lieu-
tenants were yet to be chosen. One after
another—first, second, and *brevet*—was proposed, balloted for, and elected in the same
way as the captain.

Then there was a choice of sergeants and
corporals, till the organisation was pronounced
complete. In fine, fell a shower of congratu-
lations, with " drinks all round," and for
several successive rounds. Patriotic speeches
also, in the true " spread-eagle " style, with
applauding cheers, and jokes about Santa
Anna and his *cork*-leg ; when the company at

length separated, after singing the " Star-
Spangled Banner ".

CHAPTER IV.

AN INVITATION TO SUPPER.

LORENCE KEARNEY, parting from his new friends, the filibusters, sauntered forth upon the street.

On reaching the nearest corner he came to a stop, as if undecided which way to turn.

Not because he had lost his way. His hotel was but three blocks off; and he had, during his short sojourn in the Cresent City, become acquainted with almost every part of it. It was not ignorance of the locality, therefore, which was causing him to hesitate; but something very different, as the train of his thoughts will tell.

"Don Ignacio, at least, will expect me— wish me to come, whether she do or not. I accepted his invitation, and cannot well—oh! had I known what I do now—seen what I saw this morning——. Bah! I shall return to the hotel and never more go near her!"

But he did not return to his hotel; instead, still stood irresolute, as if the thing were worth further considering.

What made the young man act thus? Simply a belief that Luisa Valverde did not love him: and, therefore, would not care to have him as a companion at supper; for it was to supper her father had asked him. On the day before he had received the invitation, and signified acceptance of it. But he had seen

something since which had made him half
repent having done so; a man, Carlos Santander,
standing beside the woman he loved, bending
over her till his lips almost touched her forehead, whispering words that were heard and to
all appearance heeded.   What the words were
Florence Kearney knew not, but could easily
guess their nature.   They could only be of
love; for he saw the carmine on her cheeks as
she listened to them.

He had no right to call the young lady to
an account.   During all his intercourse with
Don Ignacio, he had seen the daughter scarce
half-a-score times; then only while passing out
and in—to or from his lessons.   Now and then
a few snatches of conversation had occurred
between them upon any chance theme—the
weather—the study he was prosecuting (how
he wished *she* had been his teacher)—and
the peculiarities of the New Orleans life, to

which they were both strangers. And only
once had she appeared to take more than an
ordinary interest in his speech. This, when
he talked of Mexico, and having come from his
own far land—" Irlandesa "—with an enthusi-
astic desire to visit hers, telling her of his
intention to do so. On this occasion he had
ventured to speak of what he had heard about
Mexican banditti; still more of the beauty of the
Mexican ladies—naïvely adding that he would
no doubt be in less danger of losing his life
than his heart.

To this he thought she had listened, or
seemed to listen with more than ordinary attention, looking pensive as she made reply.

"Yes, Don Florencio! you will see much in
in Mexico likely to give you gratification.
'Tis true indeed that many of my country-
women are fair—some very fair. Among them
you will soon forget——"

Kearney's heart beat wildly, hoping he would hear the monosyllable "me". But the word was not spoken. In its place the phrase "us poor exiles," with which somewhat commonplace remark the young Mexicana concluded her speech.

And still there was something in what she had said, but more in her manner of saying it, which made pleasant impression upon him— something in her tone that touched a chord already making music in his heart. If it did not give him surety of her love, it, for the time, hindered him from despairing of it.

All this had occurred at an interview he had with her only the day before; and, since, sweet thoughts and hopes were his. But on the same morning they were shattered—crushed out by the spectacle he had witnessed, and the interpretation of those whispered words he had failed to hear. It had chased all hope out of his heart, and sent him in wild aimless strides along the street, just in the right frame of mind for being caught by that call which had attracted his eyes on the poster—

"VOLUNTEERS FOR TEXAS."

And just so had he been caught; and, as described, entered among the filibustering band to be chosen its chief.

To the young Irishman it was a day of strange experiences, varying as the changes of a kaleidoscope; more like a dream than reality; and after reflecting upon it all, he thus interrogated himself—

"Shall I see her again, or not? Why not? If she's lost, she cannot be worse lost by my having another interview with her. Nor could I feel worse than I do now. Ah! with this laurel fresh placed upon my brow! What if I tell her of it—tell her I am about to enter her native land as an invader? If she care for her country that should spite her; and if I find she cares not for me, her spite would give give me pleasure."

It was not an amiable mood for a lover contemplating a visit to his sweetheart. Still, natural enough under the circumstances; and Florence Kearney, wavering no longer, turned his steps towards that part of the city where dwelt Don Ignacio Valverde.

CHAPTER V.

A STUDIED INSULT.

N a small house of the Third Municipality, in the street called *Casa Calvo*, dwelt Don Ignacio Valverde. It was a wooden structure—a frame dwelling —of French-Creole fashion, consisting of but a single story, with casement windows that opened on a verandah, in the Southern States termed *piazza;* this being but little elevated above the level of the outside street. Besides

Don Ignacio and his daughter but one other
individual occupied the house—their one only
servant, a young girl of Mexican nativity and
mixed blood, half white half Indian—in short,
a *mestiza*. The straitened circumstances of
the exile forbade a more expensive establishment. Still the insignia within were not those
of pinched poverty. The sitting-room, if small
was tastefully furnished, while among other
chattels, speaking of refinement, were several
volumes of books, a harp and a guitar, with
accompaniment of sheets of music. The strings
of these instruments Luisa Valverde knew how
to touch with the skill of a professional, both
being common in her own country.

On that night, when the election of the filibustering officers was being held in Poydras-
street, her father, alone with her in the same
sitting-room, asked her to play the harp to the
accompaniment of a song. Seating herself to

the instrument she obeyed; singing one of those *romanzas* in which the language of Cervantes is so rich. It was, in fact, the old song "El Travador," from which has been filched the music set to Mrs. Norton's beautiful lay, "Love not". But on this night the spirit of the Mexican senorita was not with her song. Soon as it was finished, and her father had become otherwise engaged, she stepped out of the room, and, standing in the piazza, glanced through the trellised lattice-work that screened it from the street. She evidently expected some one to come that way. And as her father had invited Florence Kearney to supper, and she knew of it, it would look as if he were the expected one.

If so, she was disappointed for a time, though a visitor made his appearance. The door bell, pulled from the outside, soon after summoned Pepita, the Mexican servant, to the front, and presently a heavy footfall on the wooden steps of the porch, told of a man stepping upon the piazza.

Meanwhile, the young lady had returned within the room; but the night being warm, the hinged casement stood ajar, and she could see through it the man thus entering. An air of disappointment, almost chagrin, came over her countenance, as the moonlight disclosed to her view the dark visage of Carlos Santander.

"*Pasa V. adientro, Senor Don Carlos,*" said her father also recognising their visitor through the casement; and in a moment after the Creole stepped into the room, Pepita placing a chair for him.

"Though," continued Don Ignacio, "we did not expect to have the honour of your company this evening, you are always welcome."

Notwithstanding this polite speech, there was a certain constraint or hesitancy in the way it was spoken that told of some insincerity. It was evident that on that night at least Don Carlos' host looked upon him in the light of an intruder. Evidence of the same was still more marked on the countenance, as in the behaviour of Don Ignacio's daughter. Instead of a smile to greet the new comer, something like a frown sat upon her beautiful brow, while every now and then a half angry flash from her large liquid eyes, directed towards him, might have told him he was aught but welcome. Clearly it was not for him she had several times during the same night passed out into the piazza and looked through its lattice work.

In truth, both father and daughter seemed disturbed by Santander's presence, both expecting one whom, for different reasons, they did not desire him to meet. If the Creole noticed their repugnance he betrayed no sign of it. Don Carlos Santander, besides being physically handsome, was a man of rare intellectual strength, with many accomplishments, among others the power of concealing his thoughts under a mask of imperturbable coolness. Still on this night his demeanour was different from its wont. He looked flurried and excited, his eyes scintillating as with anger at some affront lately offered him, and the sting of which still rankled in his bosom. Don Ignacio noticed this, but said nothing. Indeed he seemed to stand in awe of his guest, as though under some mysterious influence. So was he, and here it may as well be told. Santander, though by birth an American and a native of New Orleans, was of Mexican parentage, and still regarded himself as a citizen of the country of his ancestors. Only to his very intimates was it known that he held a high place in the confidence of Mexico's Dictator. But Don Ignacio knew this, and rested certain hopes upon it. More than once had Santander, for motives that will presently appear, hinted to him the possibility of a return to his own land, with restoration of the estates he had forfeited. And the exiled patriot, wearied with long waiting, was at length willing to lend an ear to conditions, which, in other days, he might have spurned as humiliating if not actually dishonourable.

It was to talk of these Santander had now presented himself; and his host suspecting it, gave the young lady a side look as much as to say, "Leave the room, Luisita".

She was but too glad to obey. Just then she preferred a turn upon the piazza ; and into this she silently glided, leaving her father alone with the guest who had so inopportunely intruded.

It is not necessary to repeat what passed between the two men. Their business was to bring to a conclusion a compact they had already

talked of, though only in general terms. It
had reference to the restitution of Don Ignacio's
confiscated estates, with, of course, also the
ban of exile being removed from him. The
price of all this, the hand of his daughter given
to Carlos Santander. It was the Creole who
proposed these terms, and insisted upon them,
even to the humiliation of himself. Madly in
love with Luisa Valverde, he suspected that on
her side there was no reciprocity of the
passion. But he would have her hand if he
could not her heart.

On that night the bargain was not destined
to reach a conclusion, their conference being
interrupted by the tread of booted feet, just
ascending the front steps, and crossing the
floor of the piazza. This followed by an exchange of salutations, in which the voice of
Luisa Valverde was heard mingling with that
of a man.

Don Ignacio looked more troubled than surprised. He knew who was there. But when the words spoken outside reached the ears of Carlos Santander, first, in openly exchanged salutations and then whispers seemingly secret and confidential, he could no longer keep his seat, but springing up, exclaimed—

"*Carrai!* It's that dog of an *Irlandes!*"

"Hish!" continued his host. "The Señor Florencio will hear you."

"I wish him to hear me. I repeat the expression, and plainly in his own native tongue. I call him a cur of an Irishman."

Outside was heard a short, sharp ejaculation, as of a man startled by some sudden surprise. It was followed by an appealing speech, this in the softer accents of a woman. Then the casement was drawn abruptly open showing two faces outside. One that of Florence

Kearney set in an angry frown; the other
Luisa Valverde's pale and appealing. An
appeal idle and too late as she herself saw.
The air had become charged with the electri-
city of deadliest anger, and between the two
men a collision was inevitable.

Without waiting for a word of invitation,
Kearney stepped over the casement sill, and
presented himself inside the room. Don
Ignacio and the Creole were by this also on
their feet; and for a second or so the three
formed a strange triangular tableau — the
Mexican with fear on his face, that of Santander still wearing the expression of insult,
as when he had exclaimed, "Cur of an Irishman!" Kearney confronting him with a look
of indignant defiance.

There was an interval of silence, as that of
calm preceding storm. It was broken by the
guest latest arrived saying a few words to his

host, but in calm, dignified tone; an apology for having unceremoniously entered the
room.

"No need to apologise," promptly rejoined
Don Ignacio. "You are here by my invitation, Señor Don Florencio, and my humble
home is honoured by your presence."

The Hidalgo blood pure in Valverde's veins,
had boiled up at seeing a man insulted under
his roof.

"Thanks," said the young Irishman.

"And now, sir," he continued, turning to
Santander and regarding him with a look of
recovered coolness, "having made *my* apology,
I require *yours*".

"For what?" asked Santander, counter-
feiting ignorance.

"For using language that belongs to the
bagnios of New Orleans, where, I doubt not,
you spend most part of your time."

Then, suddenly changing tone and expression of face, he added—

"Cur of a Creole! you must take back your words?"

"Never! It's not my habit to take, but to give; and to you I give this!"

So saying, he stepped straight up to the Irishman, and spat in his face.

Kearney's heart was on fire. His hand was already on the butt of his pistol; but, glancing behind, he saw that pale appealing face, and with an effort restrained himself, calmly saying to Santander:

"Calling yourself a gentleman, you will no doubt have a card and address. May I ask you to favour me with it, as to-morrow I shall have occasion to write to you? If a scoundrel such as you can boast of having a friend, you may as well give him notice he will be needed. Your card, sir!"

"Take it!" hissed the Creole, flinging his card on the table. Then glaring around, as if his glance would annihilate all, he clutched hold of his hat, bowed haughtily to Don Ignacio, looked daggers at his daughter, and strode out into the street.

Though to all appearance defeated and humbled, he had in truth succeeded in his design, one he had long planned and cherished to bring about, a duel with Kearney in which his antagonist should be challenger. This would give him the choice of weapons, which, as he well knew, would ensure to him both safety and success. Without the certainty of this, Carlos Santander would have been the last man to provoke such an encounter; for, with all his air of *bravache*, he was the veriest of cowards.

4

CHAPTER VI.

"TO THE SALUTE!"

HE thick "swamp-fog" still hovered above the Crescent City, when a carriage drawn by two horses rolled out through one of its suburbs, and on along the Shellroad, and in the direction of Lake Pontchartrian.

It was a close carriage—a hackney—with two men upon the driver's seat and three inside. Of these last, one was Captain Florence Kearney and another Lieutenant Francis Crittenden, both officers of the filibustering band, with titles not two days old. Now on the way neither to Texas nor Mexico, but to the shore of Lake Pontchartrian, where many an affair of honour has been settled by the spilling of much blood. A stranger in New Orleans, and knowing scarce a soul, Kearney had bethought him of the young fellow who had been elected first lieutenant, and asked him to act as his second. Crittenden, a Kentuckian, being one of those who could not only stand fire, but *eat* it, if the occasion called, eagerly responded to the appeal; and they were now *en route* along the Shell road to meet Carlos Santander and whoever he might have with him.

The third individual inside the carriage belonged to that profession, and one of whose members usually makes the third in a duel—

the doctor. He was a young man who, in the capacity of surgeon, had attached himself to the band of filibusters.

Besides the mahogany box balanced upon his thigh, there was another lying on the spare bit of cushion beside him, opposite to where Crittenden sat. It was of a somewhat different shape; and no one who had ever seen a case of duelling pistols could mistake it for aught else—for it was such.

As it had been arranged that swords were to be the weapons, and a pair of these were seen in a corner of the carriage, what could they be wanting with pistols?

It was Kearney who put this question; now for the first time noticing what seemed to him a superfluous armament. It was asked of Crittenden to whom the pistols belonged; as might have been learnt by looking at his name engraved on the indented silver plate.

"Well," answered the Kentuckian; "I'm no great swordsman myself. I usually prefer pistols, and thought it may be as well to bring a pair along. I didn't much like the look of your antagonist's friend, and it's got into my head that before leaving the ground I may have something to say to *him* on my own account. So if it come to that I shall take to the barkers."

Kearney smiled, but said nothing, feeling satisfied that in case of any treachery, he had the right sort of man for his second.

He might have felt further secure, in a still other supporting party, who rode on the box beside the driver. This was a man carrying a a long rifle, that stood with the barrel two feet above his shoulders, and the butt rested between his heavily booted feet.

It was Cris Rock who had insisted on coming along as he said, to see that the fight was all "fair and squar". He too had conceived an unfavourable opinion of both the men to be met, from what he had seen of them at the rendezvous; for Santander's second had also been there. With the usual caution of one accustomed to fighting Indians, he always went armed, and usually with his long "pea" rifle.

On reaching a spot of open ground alongside the road and near the shore of the lake, the carriage stopped. It was the place of the appointed meeting as arranged by the seconds on the preceding day.

Though their antagonists had not yet arrived, Kearney and Crittenden got out, leaving the young surgeon busied with his cutlery and bandage apparatus.

"I hope you won't have to use them, doctor," remarked Kearney, with a light laugh, as he sprang out of the carriage. "I don't want you to practice upon me till we've made conquest of Mexico."

"And not then, I trust," soberly responded the surgeon.

Crittenden followed, carrying the swords; and the two leaping across the drain which separated the road from the duelling ground, took stand under a tree.

Rock remained firm on the coach box still seated and silent. As the field was full under his view, and within range of his rifle, he knew that, like the doctor, he would be near enough if wanted.

Ten minutes passed—most of the time in solemn silence, on the part of the principal, with some anxious thoughts. No matter how courageous a man may be—however skilled in weapons, or accustomed to the deadly use of them—he cannot, at such a crisis, help having a certain tremor of the heart, if not a misgiving of conscience. He has come there to kill, or be killed; and the thought of either should be sufficient to disturb mental equanimity. At such times he who is not gifted with natural courage had needs have a good cause, and confidence in the weapon to be used. Florence Kearney possessed all three; and though it was his first appearance in a duel, he had no fear for the result. Even the still sombre scene, with the long gray moss, hanging down from the dark cypress trees like the drapery of a hearse, failed to inspire him with dread. If at times a slight nervousness came over him it was instantly driven off by the thought of the insult he had received—and perhaps, also, a little by the remembrance of those dark eyes he fancied would flash proudly if he triumphed, and weep bitterly were he to suffer discomfiture. Very different were his feelings now from those he experienced less than forty-eight hours before,

when he was on his way to the house of Don
Ignacio Valverde. That night before leaving
it, he was good as sure he possessed the heart
of Don Ignacio's daughter. Indeed she had all
but told him so; and was this not enough to
nerve him for the encounter near at hand?

Very near now—close to commencing. The
rumbling of wheels heard through the drooping
festoonery of the trees, proclaimed that a second
carriage was approaching along the Shell road.
It could only be that containing the antagonists.
And it was that. In less than ten minutes
after it drew up on the causeway about twenty
paces to the rear of the one already arrived.
Two men got out, who although wrapped in
cloaks and looking as large as giants through
the thick mist could be recognised as Carlos
Santander and his second. There was a third
individual, who, like the young surgeon, remained by the carriage—no doubt a doctor,

too,—making the duelling party symmetrical
and complete.

Santander and his friend having pulled off
their cloaks and tossed them back into the
carriage, turned towards the wet ditch, and
also leaped over it.

The first performed the feat somewhat awk-
wardly, drooping down upon the further bank
with a ponderous thud.   He was a large,
heavily built man—altogether unlike one pos-
sessing the activity necessary for a good swordsman.

His atagonist might have augured well from
his apparent clumsinesss, but for what he had
heard of him.   For Carlos Santander, though
having the repute of a swaggerer, with some
suspicion of cowardice, had proved himself a
dangerous adversary by twice killing his man.
His second—a French Creole, called Dupcron—
enjoyed a similar reputation, he, too, having

been several times engaged in affairs that re-
sulted fatally. At this period New Orleans
was emphatically the city of the *duello*—for
this speciality perhaps the most noted in the
world.

As already said, Florence Kearney knew the
sort of man he had to meet, and this being his
own first appearance in a duelling field, he
might well have been excused for feeling some
anxiety as to the result. It was so slight, however, as not to betray itself, either in his looks
or gestures. Confiding in his skill, gained by
many a set-to with buttoned foils, and sup-
ported as he was by the gallant young Kentuckian, he knew nothing that could be called
fear. Instead as his antagonist advanced towards
the spot where he was standing, and he looked
at the handsome, yet sinister face—his thoughts
at the same time reverting to Luisa Valverde,
and the insult upon him in her presence—his

nerves, not at all unsteady, now became firm as steel. Indeed the self-confident, almost jaunty air, with which his adversary came upon the ground, so far from shaking them—the effect no doubt intended—but braced them the more.

When the new comers had advanced a certain distance into the meadow, Crittenden forsaking his stand under the tree, stepped out to meet them, Kearney following a few paces behind.

A sort of quadruple bow was the exchanged salutation ; then the principals remained apart, the seconds drawing nigher to one another and entering upon the required conference.

Only a few words passed between them, as but few were required ; the weapons, distance, and mode of giving the word, having all been pre-arranged.

There was no talk of apology—nor thought

of it being either offered or accepted. By their attitude, and in their looks, both the challenged aud challenger showed a full, firm determination to fight. Duperon did not seem to care much one way or the other, and the Kentuckian was not the sort to seek conciliation —with an insult such as his captain had received calling for chastisement.

After the preliminaries were passed over, the seconds again separated—each to attend upon his principal.

The young Irishman took off his coat, and rolled back his shirt sleeves up to the elbow. Santander, on the other hand, who wore a red flannel shirt under his ample *sacque*, simply threw aside the latter, leaving the shirt sleeves as they were buttoned around the wrist.

Every body was now silent; the hackney drivers on their boxes, the doctors, the gigantic Texan, all looming large and spectral-like through the still lingering mist, while the streamers of Spanish moss hanging from the cypresses around were appropriate drapery for such a scene.

In the midst of the death-like silence a voice broke in coming from the top of a tall cypress standing near. Strange and wild, it was enough not only to startle, but awe the stoutest heart. A shrill continued cachination which, though human-like could scarce be ascribed to aught human, save the laughter of a maniac.

It frightened no one there, all knowing what it was—the cackling cry of the white-headed eagle.

As it ended, but before its echoes had ceased reverberating among the trees, another sound, equally awe-inspiring, woke the echoes of the forest further down. This the *whoo-whoo-whooa* of the great southern owl, seemingly a groan in answer to the eagle's laugh.

In all countries, and throughout all ages, the hooting of the owl has been superstitously dreaded as ominous of death, and might have dismayed our duellists, had they been men of the common kind of courage. Neither were or seemed not to be; for as the lugubrious notes were still echoing in their ears, they advanced, and with rapiers upraised, stood confronting each other, but one look on their faces, and one thought in their hearts—"*to kill!*"

CHAPTER VII.

A DUEL "TO THE DEATH".

HE duellists stood confronting one another, in the position of "salute," both hands on high grasping their swords at hilt and point, the blades held horizontally. The second of each was in his place, on the left hand of his principal, half a pace in advance. But a moment more all were waiting for the word. The second of the challenger had the right to give it, and Crittenden was not the man to make delay.

"*Engage!*" he cried out, in a firm clear voice, at the same time stepping half a pace forward, Duperon doing the same. The movement was made as a precaution against foul play; sometimes, though not always, intended. For in the excitement of such a moment, or under the impatience of angry passion, one or other of the principals may close too quickly —to prevent which is the duty of the seconds.

Quick, at the "engage," both came to "guard" with a collision that struck sparks from the steel, proving the hot anger of the adversaries. Had they been cooler, they would have crossed swords quietly. But when, the instant after, they came to *tierce*, both appeared more collected, their blades for a while keeping in contact, and gliding around each other as if they had been a single piece.

For several minutes this cautious play continued, without further sparks, or only such as appeared to scintillate from the eyes of the combatants. Then came a counterthrust, quickly followed by a counter parry, with no advantage to either.

Long ere this, an observer acquainted with the weapons they were wielding, could have seen that of the two Kearney was the better swordsman. In changing from *carte* to *tierce*, or reversely, the young Irishman showed himself possessed of the power to keep his arm straight and do the work with his wrist, whilst the Creole kept bending his elbow, thus exposing his forearm to the adversary's point.

It is a rare accomplishment among swordsmen, but when present, insuring almost certain victory, that is, other circumstances being equal.

In Kearney's case, it perhaps proved the saving of his life; since it seemed to be the sole object of his antagonist to thrust in upon him, heedless of his own guard. But the long, straight point, from shoulder far outstretched, and never for an instant obliquely, foiled all his attempts.

After a few thrusts, Santander seemed surprised at his fruitless efforts. Then over his face came a look more like fear. It was the first time in his duelling experience he had been so baffled, for it was his first encounter with an adversary who could keep a *straight arm*.

But Florence Kearney had been taught *tierce* as well as *carte*, and knew how to practice it. For a time he was prevented from trying it by the other's impetuous and incessant thrusting, which kept him continuously at guard, but as the sword-play proceeded, he began to discover the weak points of his antagonist, and, with a well-directed thrust, at length sent his blade through the Creole's outstretched arm, impaling it from wrist to elbow.

An ill-suppressed cry of triumph escaped from the Kentuckian's lips, while with eyes directed towards the other second, he seemed to ask :

"Are you satisfied ?"

Then the question was formally put.

Duperon looked in the face of his principal, though without much show of interrogating him. It seemed as if he already divined what the answer would be.

"*A la mort!*" cried the Creole, with a deadly emphasis and bitter determination in his dark sinister eyes.

"To the death be it !" was the response of the Irishman, not so calmly, and now for the first time showing anger. Nor strange he should, since he now knew he had crossed swords with a man determined on taking his life.

There was a second or two's pause, of which Santander availed himself, hastily whipping a handkerchief round his wounded arm—a permission not strictly according to the code, but tacitly granted by his gallant antagonist.

When the two again closed and came to guard, the seconds were no longer by their sides. At the words "*a la mort*" they had withdrawn—each to the rear of his principal —the mode of action in a duel to the death. Their *role* henceforth was simply to look on, with no right of interference, unless either of the principals should attempt foul play. This, however, could not well occur. By the phrase "*a la mort*" it conveyed a peculiar meaning, well-known to the New Orleans duellist. When spoken, it is no longer a question of sword-skill, or who draws first blood; but a challenge giving free licence to kill—whichever can.

In the present affair it was followed by silence more profound and more intense than ever, while the attention of the spectators, now including the seconds, seemed to redouble itself.

The only sound heard was a whistling of wings. The fog had drifted away, and several large birds were seen circling in the air above, looking down with stretched necks, as if they, too, felt interested in the spectacle passing underneath. No doubt they did; for they were vultures, and could see—whether or not they scented it—that blood was being spilled.

Once more, also, from the tree tops came the mocking laughter of the eagle; and out of the depths, through long, shadowy arcades the mournful hootings of the great white owl —fit music for such fell strife.

Disregarding these ominous sounds—each

seeming a death warning in itself—the combatants had once more closed, again and again crossing sword-blades with a clash that frighted owl, eagle, and vulture, for an instant causing them to withhold their vocal accompaniment.

Though now on both sides the contest was carried on with increased anger, there was not much outward sign of it. On neither any rash sword-play. If they had lost temper they yet had control over their weapons; and their guards and points, though perhaps more rapidly exchanged, displayed as much skill as ever.

Again Kearney felt surprised at the repeated thrusts of his antagonist, which kept him all the time on the defensive, while Santander appeared equally astonished and discomfited by that far-reaching arm, straight as a yard-stick, with elbow never bent. Could the Creole have but added six inches to his rapier bladc, in less than ten seconds the young Irishman would have had nearly so much of it passed between his ribs.

Twice its point touched, slightly scratching the skin upon his breast, and drawing blood.

For quite twenty minutes the sanguinary strife continued without any marked advantage to either. It was a spectacle somewhat painful to behold, the combatants themselves being a sight to look upon. Kearney's shirt of finest white linen, showed like a butcher's ; his sleeves encrimsoned ; his hands, too, grasping his rapier hilt, the same—not with his own blood, but that of his adversary's which had run back along the blade ; his face was spotted by the drops dashed over it from the whirling wands of steel.

Gory, too, was the face of Santander ; but gashed as well. Bending forward to put in a point, the Creole had given his antagonist a chance, resulting to himself in a punctured cheek, the scar of which would stay there for life.

It was this brought the combat to an end; or, at all events, to its concluding stroke. Santander, vain of his personal appearance, on feeling his cheek laid open, suddenly lost command of himself; and with a fierce oath rushed at his adversary regardless of the consequences.

He succeeded in making a thrust, though not the one he intended. For having aimed at Kearney's heart, missing it, his blade passed through the buckle of the young Irishman's braces, where in an instant it was entangled.

Only for half-a-second; but this was all the skilled swordsman required. Now, first since the fight began, his elbow was seen to bend. This to obtain room for a thrust, which was sent, to all appearance, home to his adversary's heart.

Everyone on the ground expected to see Santander fall; for by the force of the blow and direction Kearney's blade should have passed through his body, splitting the heart in twain. Instead, the point did not appear to penetrate even an inch! As it touched, there came a sound like the chinking of coin in a purse, with simultaneously the snap of a breaking blade, and the young Irishman was seen standing as in a trance of astonishment, in his hand but the half of a sword, the other half gleaming amongst the grass at his feet.

It seemed a mischance, fatal to Florence Kearney, and only the veriest dastard would have taken advantage of it. But this Santander was, and once more drawing back, and bringing his blade to *tierce*, he was rushing on

his now defenceless antagonist, when Crittenden called "Foul play!" at the same time
springing forward to prevent it.

His interference, however, would have been
too late, and in another instant the young
Irishman would have have been stretched lifeless along the sward, but for a second individual
who had watched the foul play—one who had
been suspecting it all along. The sword of
Santander seen flying off, as if struck out of his
grasp, and his arm dropping by his side, with
blood pouring from the tips of his fingers, were
all nearly simultaneous incidents, as also the
crack of a rifle and a cloud of blue smoke suddenly spurting up over one of the carriages, and
half concealing the colossal figure of Cris Rock,
still seated on the box. Out of that cloud
came a cry in the enraged voice of the Texan,
with words which made all plain—

"Ye darned Creole cuss! Take that for a

treetur an' a cowart ! Strip the skunk ! He's got sumthin' steely under his shirt ; I heerd the chink o' it."

Saying which he bounded down from the box, sprang over the water-ditch, and rushed on towards the spot occupied by the combatants.

In a dozen strides he was in their midst, and before either of the two seconds, equally astonished, could interfere, he had caught Santander by the throat, and tore open the breast of his shirt !

Underneath was then seen another shirt, not flannel, nor yet linen or cotton, but link-and-chain steel !

Chapter VIII.

A DISGRACED DUELLIST.

MPOSSIBLE to describe the scene which followed, or the expression upon the faces of those men who stood beside Santander. The Texan, strong as he was big, still kept hold of him, though now at arm's length; in his grasp retaining the grown man with as much apparent ease as though it were but a child. And there, sure enough, under the torn flannel shirt all could see a doublet of chain armour, impenetrable to sword's point as plate of solid steel !

Explanation this of why Carlos Santander was so ready to take the field in a duel, and had twice left his antagonist lifeless upon it. It explained also why, when leaping across the water-ditch, he had dropped so heavily upon the farther bank. Weighted as he was, no wonder.

By this time the two doctors, with the pair of hackney-drivers, seeing that something had turned up out of the common course, parting from the carriages, had also come upon the ground ; the jarveys, in sympathy with Cris Rock, crying " Shame !" In the Crescent city even a cabman has something of chivalry in his nature—the surroundings teach and invite it— and now the detected scoundrel seemed without a single friend. For he—hitherto acting as such, seeing the imposture, which had been alike practised on himself, stepped up to his principal, and looking him scornfully in the face, hissed out the word " *Lâche !* "

Then turning to Kearney and Crittenden he added :

" Let that be my apology to you, gentlemen. If you're not satisfied with it, I'm willing and ready to take his place—with either of you."

" It's perfectly satisfactory, monsieur," frankly responded the Kentuckian, " so far as I'm concerned. And, I think, I may say as much for Captain Kearney."

" Indeed, yes," assented the Irishman, adding : " We absolve you, sir, from all blame. It's evident you knew nothing of that shining panoply, till now," as he spoke pointing to the steel shirt.

The French Creole haughtily but courteously, bowed thanks ; then facing once more to San-

tander, and repeating the "*Lâche*," strode
silently away from the ground.

They had all mistaken the character of the
individual, who, despite a somewhat forbidding
face, was evidently a man of honour, as he had
proved himself.

"What dye weesh me to do wi' him?" interrogated the Texan, still keeping Santander
in firm clutch. "Shed we shoot or hang him?"

"Hang!" simultaneously shouted the two
hackney drivers, who seemed as bitter against
the disgraced duellist as if he had "bilked"
them of a fare.

"So I say, too," solemnly pronounced the
Texan; "Shootin's too good for the like o' him
a man capable o' sech a cowardly, murderous
trick desarves to die the death o' a dog."

Then with an interrogating look at Crittenden, he added : "Which is't to be, lootenant?"

"Neither, Cris"; answered the Kentuckian.

If I mistake not, the *gentleman* has had enough punishment without either. If he's got a spark of shame or conscience——."

" Conshence," exclaimed Rock, interrupting. " Sech a skunk don't know the meanin' o' the word. Darn ye !" he continued, turning upon his prisoner, and shaking him till the links in the steel shirt chinked, " I feel as if I ked drive the blade o' my bowie inter ye through them steel fixins an' all."

And drawing his knife from its sheath he brandished it in a menacing manner.

" Don't, Rock ! Please don't " interposed the Kentuckian, Kearney joining in the entreaty. " He's not worth anger, much less revenge. So let him go."

" You're right thar, lootenant," rejoined Rock. " He ain't worth eyther, that's the truth. An 'twould only be puttin' pisen on the blade o' my knife to smear it wi' his black blood.

F'r all, I aint a gwine to let him off so easy 's
all that, unless you an .the captain insists on it.
After the warmish work he's had, an the sweat
he's put himself in by the wearin' o' two shirts
at a time, I guess he won't be any the worse of
a sprinkling o' cold water.   So here goes to gie
it him."

Saying which, he strode off towards the ditch,
half-dragging, half-carrying Santander   along
with him.

The cowed and craven creature neither. made
resistance, nor dared.   Had he done so, the
upshot was obvious.   For the Texan's blade,
still bared, was shining before his eyes, and he
knew that any attempt on his part either to
oppose the latter's intention or escape, would
result in having it buried between his ribs.
So, silently, sullenly, he allowed himself to be
taken along, not as a lamb to the slaughter,
but a wolf, or rather dog, about to be chastised
for some wilful malfeasance.

In an instant after the chastisement was administered by the Texan laying hold of him with both hands, lifting him from off his feet, and then dropping him down into the water ditch, where, weighted with the steel shirt, he fell with a dead, heavy plunge, going at once to the bottom.

" That's less than your desarvins," said the Texan, on thus delivering his charge. " An' if't had been left to Cris Rock 'twould a' been *up*, stead o' *down*, he'd a sent ye. If iver man desarved hangin', you're the model o' him. Ha —ha—ha ! Look at the skunk now !"

The last words with the laugh preceding them, were elicited by the ludicrous appearance which Santander presented. He had come to the surface again, and with some difficulty, owing to the encumberance of his under-shirt, clambered out upon the bank. But not as when he went under. Instead, with what ap-

peared a green cloak over his shoulders, the
scum of the stagnant water long collecting un-
disturbed.

The hackney driver—there was but one now,
the other taken off by Duperon who had hired
him, their doctor too—joined with Rock in his
laughter, while Kearney, Crittenden, and their
own surgeon could not help uniting in the
chorus.   Never had tragic hero suffered a more
comical discomfiture.

He was now permitted to withdraw from the
scene of it, a permission of which he availed
himself without further delay ; first retreating
for some distance along the Shell road, as one
wandering and distraught ; then, as if seized by
a sudden thought, diving into the timbered
swamp alongside, and there disappearing.

Soon after, the carriage containing the victorious party rattled past ; they inside it scarce
casting a look to see what had become of

Santander. He was nothing to them now ; at best only a thing to be a matter of ludicrous remembrance. Nor long remained he in their thoughts ; these now reverting to Texas, and their necessity for hastening back to the Crescent City, to make start for " The Land of the Lone Star ".

CHAPTER IX.

A SPARTAN BAND.

IN ancient days Sparta had its Thermopylæ, while in those of modern date Sicily saw a thousand men in scarlet shirts make landing upon her coast, and conquer a kingdom defended by a military force twenty or thirty times their number !

But deeds of heroism are not alone confined to the history of the Old World. That of the new presents us with many pages of a similar kind, and Texas can tell of achievements not surpassed, either in valour or chivalry, by any upon record. Such was the battle of San Jacinto, where the Texans were victorious, though overmatched in the proportion of ten to one : such the defence of Fort Alamo when the brave Colonel Crockett, now world-known, surrendered up his life, alongside the equally brave " Jim Bowie," he who gave his name to the knife which on that occasion he so efficiently wielded—after a protracted and terrible struggle dropping dead upon a heap of foes who had felt its sharp point and keen edge.

Among the deeds of great renown done by the defenders of the young Republic, none may take higher rank, since none is entitled to it, than that known as the battle of Mier. Though they there lost the day—a defeat due to the incapacity of an ill-chosen leader—they won glory eternal. Every man of them who fell had

first killed his foeman—some half a score—
while of those who survived there was not one
so craven as to cry " Quarter !"   The white flag
went not up till they were overwhelmed and
overpowered by sheer disparity of numbers.

It was a fight at first with rifles and musketry
at long range ; then closer as the hostile host
came crowding in upon them ; the bullets sent
through windows and loop-holed walks—some
from the flat parapetted roofs of the houses—
till at length it became a conflict hand to hand
with knife, sword, and pistol, or guns clubbed
—being empty, with no time to reload them
—many a Texan braining one antagonist with
the butt of his piece after having sent its bullet
through the body of another !

Vain all !   Brute strength, represented by
superior numbers, triumphed over warlike
prowess, backed by indomitable courage ; and
the " Mier Expedition," from which Texas had

expected so much, ended disastrously, though ingloriously; those who survived being made prisoners and carried off to the capital of Mexico.

Of the Volunteer Corps, which composed this ill-fated expedition—and they were indeed all volunteers—none gave better account of itself than that organised in Poydras-street, New Orleans, and among its individual members no man behaved than he whom they had chosen as their leader. Florence Kearney had justified their choice and proved true to the trust, as all who outlived that fatal day ever after admitted. Fortunately he himself was among the survivors; by a like good luck, so too were his first-lieutenant Crittenden and Cris Rock. As at "Fanning's Massacre," so at Mier the gigantic Texan performed prodigies of valour, laying around him, and slaying on all sides, till at length wounded and disabled, like a

lion beset by a *cheavux-de-frise* of Caffre
assegais, he was compelled to submit. Fighting side by side, with the man he had first
taken a fancy to on the Levee of New Orleans,
and afterwards became instrumental in making
captain of his corps—finding this man to be
what he had conjecturally believed and pronounced him—of the "true grit"—Cris Rock
now felt for Florence Kearney almost the
affection of a father, combined with the grand
respect which one gallant soul is ever ready to
pay another. Devotion, too, so strong and
real, that had the young Irishman called upon
him for the greatest risk of his life, in any
good or honourable cause, he would have responded to the call without a moment's hesitancy
or murmur. Nay, more than risk; he would
have laid it down, absolutely, to save that of
his cherished leader.

Proof of this was, in point of fact, afforded

but a short while after. Any one acquainted with Texan history will remember how the Mier prisoners, while being taken to the city of Mexico, rose upon their guards and mastering them, made their escape to the mountains around. This occurred at the little town of El Salado, and was caused by the terrible sufferings the captives had endured upon the march, added to many insults and cruelties, to which they had been subjected, not only by the Mexican soldiers, but the officers having them in charge. These had grown altogether unsupportable, at El Salado reaching the climax.

It brought about the crisis for a long time accumulating; and which the Texans anticipated. For they had, at every opportunity afforded them, talked over and perfected a plan of escape.

By early daybreak on a certain morning, as their guards were carelessly lounging about an idle hour before continuing that toilsome journey—a signal shout was heard.

"Now boys; up and at them!" were the words, with some others following, which all well understood—almost a repetition of the famous order of Wellington at Waterloo. And as promptly obeyed; for on hearing it the Texans rushed at the soldiers of the escort, wrenched from them their weapons, and with those fought their way through the hastily-formed ranks of the enemy out into the open country.

So far they had succeeded, though in the end, for most of them, it proved a short and sad respite. Pursued by an overwhelming force—fresh troops drawn from the garrisons in the neighbourhood, added to the late escort so shamefully discomfited, and smarting under the humiliation and defeat—the pursuit carrying them through a country to which they were entire strangers—a district almost uninhabited, without roads, and, worse still, without water,—not strange that all, or nearly all, of them were recaptured, and carried back to El Salado.

Then ensued a scene worthy of being enacted by savages, for little better than savages were those in whose custody they were. Exulting fiendlike over their recapture, at first the word went round that all were to be executed; this being the general wish of their captors. No doubt the deed of wholesale vengeance would have been done, and our hero, Florence Kearney, with his companion Cris Rock, never more have been heard of; in other words, the novel of the "Free Lances" would not have been written. But among those reckless avengers there were some who knew better than to advocate indiscriminate slaughter. It was " a far cry to Loch Awe," all knew; the Highland loch typified not by Texas, but the United States. But the more knowing ones always knew that, however far, the cry might be heard, and then what the result? No mere band of Texan filibusters, ill-organised, and but poorly equipped, to come across the Rio Grande; instead a well-disciplined army in numbers enough for sure retaliation, bearing the banner of the "Stars and Stripes".

In fine, a more merciful course was determined upon ; only *decimation* of the prisoners —every tenth man to suffer death.

There was no word about degrees in their guiltiness—all were alike in this respect— and the fate of each was to be dependent on pure blind chance.

When the retaken escapadoes had been brought back to El Salado, they were drawn up in line of single file, and carefully counted. A helmet, snatched from the head of one of the dragoons guarding them, was made use of as a ballot box. Into this were thrown a number of what we call French or kidney beans—the *pijoles* of Mexico—in count corresponding to that of the devoted victims. Of these *pijoles* there are several varieties, distinguishable chiefly by their colour. Two sorts are common, the black and white; and these were chosen to serve as tickets in that dread lottery of life and death. For every nine white beans there was a black one; he who drew black would be shot within the hour!

Into the hard soldier's head-piece, appropriate for such purpose, the beans were dropped, and the drawing done as designed. I, who now write of it long after, can truthfully affirm that never in the history of human kind has there been a grander exhibition of man's courage than was that day given at El Salado. The men who exemplified it were of no particular nation. As a matter of course, the main body of the Texans were of American birth, but among them were also Englishmen, Scotchmen, Irishmen, French, and Germans—even some who spoke Spanish, the language of their captors, now their judges, and about to become their executioners. But when that helmet of horrible contents was carried round, and held before each, not one showed the slightest fear or hesitancy to plunge his hand into it, though knowing that what they should bring up between their fingers might be the sealing of their fate. Many laughed and made laughter among their comrades, by some quaint *jeu d'esprit*. One reckless fellow—no other than Cris Rock—as he fearlessly rattled the beans about, cried aloud :

"Wal, boys; I guess it's the tallest gamblin' I've ever took a hand at. But this child aint afeerd. I was born to good luck, an' am not likely to go under—jest yet."

The event justified his confidence, as he drew *blank*—not *black*, the fatal colour.

It was now Kearney's turn to undergo the dread ordeal; and, without flinching, he was about to insert his hand into the helmet, when the Texan, seizing hold of it, stayed him.

" No, cap. !" he exclaimed ; " I'm wownded, putty bad, as ye see "—(he had received a lance thrust in their struggle with the guards) —"an' mayent git over it. Thurfor, your life's worth more'n mine. Besides, my luck's good jest now. So let me take your chance. That's allowed, as these skunks hev sayed themselves."

So it was—a declaration having been made by the officer who presided over the drawing —from humane motives as pretended—that any one who could find a substitute might himself stand clear. A grim mockery it seemed ; and yet it was not so ; since, besides Cris Rock, more than one courageous fellow

7

proposed the same to comrade and friend—in
the case of two brothers the elder one insisting
upon it.

Though fully, fervently appreciating the
generous offer, Florence Kearney was not the
man to avail himself of it.

"Thanks, brave comrade!" he said, with
warmth, detaching his hand from the Texan's
grasp, and thrusting it into the helmet.
"What's left of your life yet is worth more
than all mine; and my luck may be good as
yours—we'll see."

It proved so, a murmur of satisfaction running along the line as they saw his hand drawn
out with a white bean between the fingers.

"Thanks to the Almighty!" joyously
shouted the Texan, as he made out the colour.
"Both o' us clar o' that scrape, by Job! An'
as there aint no need for me dyin' yet, I mean
to live it out, an' git well agin."

And get well he did, despite the long after march, with all its exposures and fatigues; his health and strength being completely restored as he stepped over the threshold, entering within his prison cell in the City of Mexico.

与 with all its exposure and distress
...ab... as being carried by men...

CHAPTER X.

THE ACORDADA.

NE of the most noted "lions" in the City of Mexico is the prison called La Acordada. Few strangers visit the Mexican capital without also paying a visit to this celebrated penal establishment, and few who enter its gloomy portals issue forth from them without having seen something to sadden the heart, and be ever afterwards remembered with repugnance and pain.

There is, perhaps, no prison in the universal
world where one may witness so many, and
such a variety of criminals ; since there is no
crime known to the calendar that has not been
committed by some one of the gaol-birds of
the Acordada.

Its cells, or cloisters—for the building was
once a monastery—are usually well filled with
thieves, forgers, ravishers, highway robbers,
and a fair admixture of murderers ; none
appearing cowed or repentant, but boldly
brazening it out, and even boasting of their
deeds of villany, fierce and strong as when
doing them, save the disabled ones, who suffer
from wounds or some loathsome disease.

Nor is all their criminal action suspended
inside the prison walls. It is carried on
within their cells, and still more frequently in
the court-yards of the ancient convent, where
they are permitted to meet in common and

spend a considerable portion of their time. Here they may be seen in groups, most of them ragged and greasy, squatted on the flags, card-playing—and cheating when they can— now and then quarrelling, but always talking loud and cursing.

Into the midst of this mass of degraded humanity were thrust two of the unfortunate prisoners, taken at the battle of Mier—the two with whom our tale has alone to do.

For reasons that need not be told most of the captives were excepted from this degradation; the main body of them being carried on through the city to the pleasant suburban village of Tacubaya.

But Florence Kearney and Cris Rock were not among the exceptions; both having been consigned to the horrid pandemonium we have painted.

It was some consolation to them that they

were allowed to share the same cell, though they would have liked it better could they have had this all to themselves. As it was, they had not; two individuals being bestowed in it along with them.

It was an apartment of but limited dimensions—about eight feet by ten—the cloister of some ancient monk, who, no doubt, led a jolly enough life of it there, or, if not there, in the refectory outside, in the days when the Acordada was a pleasant place of residence for himself and his cowled companions. For his monastery, as "Bolton Abbey in the olden time," saw many a scene of good cheer, its inmates being no anchorites.

Besides the Texan prisoners, its other occupants now were men of Mexican birth. One of them, under more favourable circumstances, would have presented a fine appearance. Even in his prison garb, somewhat ragged and squalid, he looked the gentleman and something more. For there was that in his air and physiognomy, which proclaimed him no common man. Captivity may hold and make more fierce, but cannot degrade the, lion. And just as a lion in its cage seemed this man in a cell of the Acordada. His face was of the rotund type, bold in its expression, yet with something of gentle humanity, seen when searched for, in the profound depths of a dark penetrating eye. His complexion was a clear olive, such as is common to Mexicans of pure Spanish descent, the progeny of the Conquistadors; his beard and moustache coal-black, as also the thick mass of hair that, bushing out and down over his ears, half concealed them.

Cris Rock "cottoned" to this man on sight. Nor liked him much the less when told he had been a robber! Cris supposed that in Mexico a robber may sometimes be an honest man, or at all events, have taken to the road through some supposed wrong—personal or political. Freebooting is less a crime, or at all events, more easy of extenuation in a country whose chief magistrate himself is a freebooter; and such, at this moment, neither more nor less, was the chief magistrate of Mexico, Don Antonio Lopez de Santa Anna.

Beyond the fact, or it might be only suspicion, that Ruperto Rivas was a robber, little seemed to be known of him among the inmates of the Acordada. He had been there only a short while, and took no part in their vulgar, common-place ways of killing time; instead staying within his cell. His name had, however, leaked out, and this brought up in the minds of some of his fellow prisoners certain reminiscences pointing to him as one of the road fraternity; no common one either, but the chief of a band of "salteadores".

Altogether different was the fourth personage, entitled to a share in the cell appropriated to Kearney and Cris Rock; unlike the reputed robber as the Satyr to Hyperion. In short a contrast of the completest kind, both physically and mentally. No two beings claiming to be of human kind could have presented a greater dissimilarity—being very types of the extreme. Ruperto Rivas, despite the shabby habiliments in which the gaol authorities had arrayed him, looked all dignity and grandeur, while El Zorillo—the little fox, as his prison companions called him—was an epitomised impersonation of wickedness and meanness; not only crooked in soul, but in body—being in point of fact an *enano* or dwarf hunchback.

Previous to the arrival of those who were henceforth to share their cell, this ill-assorted pair had been kept chained together, as much

by way of punishment as to prevent escape.
But now, the gaol governor, as if struck by
a comical idea, directed them to be separated,
and the dwarf linked to the Texan Colossus
—thus presenting a yet more ludicrous contrast of couples—while the ex-captain of the
filibusters and the reputed robber were consigned to the same chain.

Of the new occupants of the cloister,
Cris Rock was the more disgusted with the
situation. His heart was large enough to
feel sympathy for humanity in any shape,
and he would have pitied his deformed fellow-
prisoner, but for a deformity of the latter
worse than any physical ugliness ; for the
Texan soon learnt that the hideous creature,
whose couch as well as chain he was forced
to share, had committed crimes of the most
atrocious nature, among the rest murder !
It was, in fact, for this last that he was now

in the Acordada—a cowardly murder, too—
a case of poisoning. That he still lived was
due to the proofs not being legally satisfactory, though no one doubted of his having
perpetrated the crime.

At first contact with this wretch the Texan
had recoiled in horror, without knowing aught
of his past. There was that in his face which
spoke a history of dark deeds. But when this
became known to the new denizens of the cell,
the proximity of such a monster was positively
revolting to them.

Vengeance itself could not have devised a
more effective mode of torture. Cris Rock
groaned under it, now and then grinding his
teeth and stamping his feet, as if he could have
trodden the misshapen thing into a still more
shapeless mass under the heels of his heavy
boots.

For the first two days of their imprisonment

in the Acordada neither of the Texans could understand why they were being thus punished —as it were to satisfy some personal spite. None of the other Mier prisoners, of whom several had been brought to the same gaol, were submitted to a like degradation. True, these were also chained two and two; but to one another, and not to Mexican criminals. Why, then, had they alone been made an exception? For their lives neither could tell or guess, though they gave way to every kind of conjecture. It was true enough that Cris Rock had been one of the ringleaders in the rising at El Salado, while the young Irishman had also taken a prominent part in that affair. Still there were others now in the Acordada who had done the same, receiving treatment altogether different. The attack upon the guards, therefore, could scarce be the cause of what they were called upon to suffer now; for besides the humiliation of being chained to criminals, they were otherwise severely dealt with. The food set before them was of the coarsest, with a scarcity of it ; and more than once the gaoler, whose duty it was to look after them, made mockery of their irksome situation, jesting on the grotesque companionship of the dwarf and giant. As the gaol governor had shown, on his first having them conveyed to their cells, signs of a special hostility, so did their daily attendant. But for what reason neither Florence Kearney, nor his faithful comrade, could divine.

They learnt it at length—on the third day after their entrance within the prison. All was explained by the door of their cell being drawn open, exposing to view the face and figure of a man well known to them. And from both something like a cry escaped, as they saw standing without, by the side of the gaol governor—Carlos Santander.

Chapter XI.

A COLONEL IN FULL FEATHER.

ES ; outside the door of their cell was Carlos Santander. And in full war panoply, wearing a magnificent uniform, with a glittering sword by his side, and on his head a cocked hat, surmounted by a *panache* of white ostrich feathers !

To explain his presence there, and in such guise, it is necessary to return upon time and state some particulars of this man's life not yet before the reader. As already said, he was a native of New Orleans, but of Mexican parentage, and regarding himself as a Mexican citizen. Something more than a mere citizen, indeed ; as previous to his encounter with Florence Kearney he had been for a time resident in Mexico, holding some sort of appointment under that Government, or from the Dictator himself —Santa Anna. What he was doing in New Orleans no one exactly knew, though among his intimates there was an impression that he still served his Mexican master, in the capacity of a secret agent—a sort of *procurador*, or spy. Nor did this suspicion do him wrong ; for he was drawing pay from Santa Anna, and doing work for him in the States, which could scarce be dignified with the name of diplomacy. Proof of its vile character is afforded by the action he took among the volunteers in Poydras-Street. His presenting himself at their rendezvous, getting enrolled in the corps, and offering as a candidate for the captaincy, were all done under instructions, and with a design which, for wickedness and cold-blooded atrocity, was worthy of Satan himself. Had he succeeded in becoming the leader of this ill-fated band, for them the upshot might have been no worse ; though it would not have been better ; since it was his intention to betray them to the enemy at the first opportunity that should offer. Thwarted in this intent ; knowing he could no longer show his face among the filibusters, even though it were but as a private in the ranks ; fearing furthermore the shame that awaited him in New Orleans soon as the affair of the steel shirt should get bruited about, he had hastily decamped from that place and, as we now know, once more made his way to Mexico.

Luckily for him, the shirt, or rather under-

8

shirt, business leaked not out ; at least not to reach the ears of anyone in the Mexican capital.

Nor, indeed, was it ever much known in New Orleans. His second, Duperon, for his own sake not desiring to make it public, had refrained from speaking of it ; and their doctor, a close little Frenchman, controlled by Duperon, remained equally reticent ; while all those on the other side—Kearney, Crittenden, Rock and the surgeon—had taken departure for Texas on the very day of the duel ; from that time forward having " other fish to fry ".

But there were still the two hackney drivers, who, no doubt, had they stayed in the Crescent city in the pursuit of their daily avocation, would have given notoriety to an occurrence, curious as it was scandalous.

It chanced, however, that both the Jarveys were Irishmen ; and suddenly smitten with warlike aspirations—either from witnessing the spectacle of the duel, or the gallant behaviour of their young countryman—on that same day dropped the ribbons, and, taking to a musket instead, were among the men who composed the ill-started expedition which came to grief on the Rio Grande.

So, for the time, Carlos Santander had escaped the brand of infamy due to his dastardly act.

His reappearance on the scene in such grand garb needs little explanation. A fairly brave and skilled soldier, a vainer man than General Antonio Lopez de Santa Anna never wore sword, and one of his foibles was to see himself surrounded by a glittering escort. The officers of his staff were very peacocks in their gaudy adornment, and as a rule the best looking of them were his first favourites. Santander on returning to Mexico, was appointed one of his aides-de-camp, and being just the sort—a showy fellow—soon rose to rank ; so that the defeated candidate for a captaincy of Texan Volunteers, was now a colonel in the Mexican Army, on the personal staff of its Commander-in-Chief.

Had Florence Kearney and Cris Rock but known they were to meet this man in Mexico —could they have anticipated seeing him, as he was now, at the door of their prison cell— their hearts would have been fainter as they toiled along the weary way, and perchance in that lottery of life and death they might have little cared whether they drew black or white.

At the sight of him there rose up all at once in their recollection that scene upon the Shell Road ; the Texan vividly recalling how he had ducked the caitiff in the ditch, as how he looked after crawling out upon the bank—mud be-draggled and covered with the viscous scum,— in strange contrast to his splendid appearance now !   And Kearney well remembered the same, noting in addition a scar on Santander's cheek—he had himself given—which the latter vainly sought to conceal beneath whiskers since permitted to grow their full length and breadth.

These remembrances were enough to make the heart of the captive Irishman beat quick, if it did not quail ; while that of the Texan had like reason to throb apprehensively.

Nor could they draw any comfort from the expression on Santander's face. Instead, they but read there what they might well believe to be their death sentence. The man was smiling, but it was the smile of Lucifer in triumph—mocking, malignant, seeming to say, without spoken word, but, for all that, emphatically and with determination,

"I have you in my power, and verily you shall feel my vengeance."

They could tell it was no accident had brought him thither, no duty of prison inspection—but the fiendish purpose to flaunt his grandeur before their eyes, and gloat over the misery he knew it would cause them. And his presence explained what had hitherto been a puzzle to them—why they two were being made an exception among their captive comrades, and thrown into such strange fellowship. It must have been to humiliate them; as, indeed, they could now tell by a certain speech which the gaol-governor addressed to Santander, as the cell door turned back upon its hinges:

"There they are, Señor Colonel! As you see, I've had them coupled according to orders. What a well-matched pair!" he added, ironically, as his eyes fell upon Cris Rock and the hunchback. "*Ay Dios!* It's a sight to draw laughter from the most sober-sided recluse that ever lodged within these walls. Ha! ha! ha!"

It drew this from Carlos Santander; who,

relishing the jest, joined in the "ha! ha!" till the old convent rang with their coarse ribaldry.

Chapter XII.

"DO YOUR DARNDEST."

URING all this time—only a few seconds it was—the four men within the cell preserved silence; the dwarf, as the door alone was drawn open, having said to the gaol governor: "*Buenas Dids Excellenza!* you're coming to set us free, an't you?"

A mere bit of jocular bravado; for, as might be supposed the deformed wretch could have little hope of deliverance, save by the gallows, to which he had actually been condemned. A creature of indomitable pluck, however, this had not so far frightened him as to hinder jesting— a habit to which he was greatly given. Besides, he did not believe he was going to the *garota*. Murderer though he was, he might expect pardon, could he only find money sufficient to pay the price, and satisfy the conscience of those who had him in keeping.

His question was neither answered nor himself taken notice of; the attention of those outside being now directed upon the other occupants of the cell. Of these only two had their faces so that they could be seen. The third who was the reputed robber, kept his turned towards the wall, the opened door being behind his back ; and this attitude he preserved, not being called upon to change it, till Santander had closed his conversation with Cris Rock

and Kearney.   He had opened it in a jaunty,
jeering tone, saying :

"Well ; my brave Filibusters !   Is this
where you are ?   *Caspita !*   In a queer place
and queer company, too !   Not so nice, Senor
Don Florencio, as that you used to keep in
the Crescent city.   And you, my Texan
Colossus !   I take it you don't find the atmosphere of the Acordada quite so pleasant as the
fresh breezes of prairieland, eh ?"

He paused, as if to note the effect of his
irony ; then continued :

"So this is the ending of the grand Mier
Expedition, with the further invasion of Mexico !   Well ; you've found your way to its
capital, anyhow; if you haven't fought it.   And
now you're here, what do you expect, pray ?"

"Not much o' good from sich a scoundrel as
you," responded Rock, in a tone of reckless
defiance.

" What ! No good from me ! An old ac-
quaintance—friend, I ought rather to call
myself, after the little scene that passed between us on the shores of Pontchartrain.
Come, gentlemen ! Being here among strangers you should think yourselves fortunate in
finding an old comrade of the filibustering
band ; one owing you so many obligations.
Ah ! well ; having the opportunity now, I shall
try my best to wipe out the indebtedness."

" You kin do your darndest," rejoined Rock
in the same sullen tone. " We don't look for
marcy at your hands nosomever. It ain't in
ye ; an if't war, Cris. Rock 'ud scorn to claim
it. So ye may do yur crowing on a dunghill,
whar there be cocks like to be scared at it.
Thar aint neery one o' that sort hyar."

Santander was taken aback by this unlooked
for rebuff. He had come to the Acordada to
indulge in the luxury of a little vapouring

over his fallen foes, whom he knew to be there, having been informed of all that had befallen them from Mier up to Mexico. He expected to find them cowed, and eager to crave life from him; which he would no more have granted than to a brace of dogs that had bitten him. But so far from showing any fear, both prisoners looked a little defiant; the Texan with the air of a caged wolf seeming ready to tear him if he showed but a step over the threshold of the cell.

" Oh ! very well," he returned, making light of what Rock had said. " If you won't accept favours from an old, and, as you know, tried friend, I must leave you so without them. But," he added addressing himself more direct-ly to Kearney :

" You, Senor Irlandes—surely you won't be so unreasonable ?"

" Carlos Santander," said the young Irishman looking his *ci-devant* adversary full in the face. " As I proved you not worth thrusting with my sword, I now pronounce you not worth words—even to call you coward— though that you are from the crown of your head to the soles of your feet. Not even brave when your body is encased in armour. Dastard ! I defy you."

Though manifestly stung by the reminder, Santander preserved his coolness. He had this, if not courage—at least a knack of feigning it. But again foiled in the attempt to humble the enemy, and moreover dreading exposure in the eyes of the gaol-governor—an old *militario*—should the story of the *steel shirt* come out in the conversation, he desisted questioning the *Tejanos.* Luckily for him none of the others there understood English— the language he and the Texans had used in their brief, but sharp exchange of words.

Now addressing himself to the governor, he said—

" As you perceive, Señor Don Pedro, these two gentlemen are old acquaintances of mine, whose present unfortunate position I regret, and would gladly relieve. Alas! I fear the law will take its course."

At which commiserating remark Don Pedro smiled grimly; well aware of the sort of interest Colonel Santander took in the pair of prisoners committed to his care. For the order so to dispose of them he knew to have come from Santander himself! It was not his place nor was he the kind of man to inquire into motives; especially when these concerned his superiors. Santander was an officer on the staff of the Dictator, besides being a favourite at Court. The gaol-governor knew it, and was subservient. Had he been commanded to secretly strangle the two men thus specially placed in his charge, or administer poison to them, he would have done it without pity or protest. The cruel tyrant who had made him governor of the Acordada knew his man, and had already, as rumour said, with history to confirm it, more than once availed himself of this means to get rid of enemies, personal or political.

During all this interlude the robber had maintained his position and silence, his face turned to the blank wall of the cloister, his back upon all the others. What his motive for this was neither of the Texans could tell ; and in all likelihood Santander knew not himself any more who the man was. But his behaviour, from its very strangeness, courted inquiry ; and seemingly struck with it, the staff-colonel, addressing himself to the gaol-governor, said :

" By the way, Don Pedro, who is your prisoner, who makes the fourth in this curious

quartette ?   He seems shy about showing his
face, which would argue it an ugly one like my
own."

A bit of badinage in which Carlos Santander
oft indulged.   He knew that he was anything
but ill-favoured as far as face went.

" Only a gentleman of the road—*un salteador*," responded the governor.

" An interesting sort of individual then,"
said Santander.   " Let me scan his countenance, and see whether it be of the true brigand
type—a Mazaroni or Diavolo."

So saying he stepped inside the cell, and
passed on till he could see over the robber's
shoulder, who now slightly turning his head,
faced towards him.   Not a word was exchanged
between the two, but from the looks it was
clear they were old acquaintances, Santander
starting as he recognised the other ; while his
glance betrayed a hostility strong and fierce as

that felt for either Florence Kearney or the Texan. A slight exclamation, involuntary, but telling of anger, was all that passed his lips as his eyes met a pair of other eyes which seemed to pierce his very heart.

He stayed not for more ; but turning upon his heel, made direct for the door. Not to reach it however without interruption. In his hurry to be gone, he stumbled over the legs of the Texan, that stretched across the cell, nearly from side to side. Angered by the obstruction he gave them a spiteful kick, then passed on outward. By good fortune fast and far out of reach, otherwise Cris Rock, who sprang to his feet, and on for the entrance, jerking the dwarf after, would in all probability, there and then have taken his life.

As it was the gaol-governor seeing the danger, suddenly shut the cloister door, so saving it.

" Jest as I've been tellin' ye all along, Cap,"

coolly remarked Rock, as the slammed door
ceased to make resonance ; " We shed a hanged
the skunk, or shot him thar an then on the
Shell Road. 'Twar a foolich thing lettin' him
out o' that ditch when I had him in it. Darn
the luck o' my not drownin' him outright !
We're like to sup sorrow for it now."

Chapter XIII.

THE EXILES RETURNED.

F the *dramatis personæ* of our tale, already known to our reader, Carlos Santander, Florence Kearney, and Cris Rock were not the only ones who had shifted residence from the City of New Orleans to that of Mexico. Within the months intervening two others had done the same—these Don Ignacio Valverde and his daughter. The banished exile had not only returned to his

native land, but his property had been restored
to him and himself reinstated in the favour of
the Dictator.

More still, he had now higher rank than ever
before ; since he had been appointed a Minister
of State.

For the first upward step on this progressive
ladder of prosperity, Don Ignacio owed all to
Carlos Santander. The handsome *aide-de-
camp*, having the ear of his chief, found little
difficulty in getting the ban removed with
leave given the refugee—criminal only in a
political sense—to come back to his country.

The motive will easily be guessed. Nothing
of either friendship or humanity actuated Santander. Alone the passion of love ; which had
to do not with Don Ignacio—but his daughter.
In New Orleans he himself dared no longer
live, and so could no more see Luisa Valverde
there. Purely personal then ; a selfish love

such as he could feel, was the motive for his
intercession with the political chief of Mexico
to pardon the political criminal. But if he had
been the means of restoring Don Ignacio to his
country, that was all. True, there was the
restitution of the exile's estates, but this followed as a consequence on reinstatement in his
political rights. The after honours and emolu-
ments—with the appointment to a seat in the
Cabinet—came from the Chief of the State,
Santa Anna himself. And his motive for thus
favouring a man who had lately, and for long,
been his political foe was precisely the same as
that which actuated Carlos Santander. The
Dictator of Mexico as famed for his gallantries
in love as his gallantry in war—and indeed
somewhat more—had looked upon Luisa Valverde, and " saw that she was fair ".

For Don Ignacio himself, as the recipient of
these favours, much may be said in extenua-

tion. Banishment from one's native land, with loss of property, and separation from friends as from best society; condemned to live in another land, where all these advantages are unattainable, amidst a companionship uncongenial; add to this the necessity of work, whether mental or physical toil, to support life—the *res augustæ domi;* sum up all these, and you have the history of Don Ignacio Valverde during his residence in New Orleans. He bore all patiently and bravely, as man could and should. For all he was willing—and it cannot be wondered at that he was—when the day came, and a letter reached him bearing the State seal of the Mexican Republic—for its insignia were yet unchanged—to say that he had received pardon, and could return home.

He knew the man who had procured it for him—Carlos Santander—and had reason to

suspect something of the motive. But the
mouth of a gift horse must not be too narrowly
examined ; and Santander, ever since that
night when he behaved so rudely in Don
Ignacio's house, had been chary in showing
his face. In point of fact, he had made but
one more visit to the Calle de Casa Calvo here,
presenting himself several days after the duel,
with a patch of court plaister on his cheek,
and his arm in a sling. An invalid, interesting
from the cause which made him an invalid, he
gave his own account of it, knowing there was
but little danger of its being contradicted.
Duperon's temper, he understood, with that of
the French doctor, securing silence. The
others were all G.T.T. (gone to Texas), the
hack-drivers, as he had taken pains to assure
himself. No fear, therefore, of what he alleged
getting denial or being called in question.

It was to the effect that he had fought

Florence Kearney, and given more and worse wounds than he himself had received—enough of them, and sufficiently dangerous ; to make it likely that his adversary would not long survive.

He did not say this to Luisa Valverde—only to her father. When she heard it second-hand, it came nigh killing her. But then the informant had gone away—perhaps luckily for himself—and could not further be questioned. When met again in Mexico months after, he told the same tale. He had no doubt, however, that his duelling adversary, so terribly gashed as to be in danger of dying, still lived. For an American paper which gave an account of the battle of Mier, had spoken of Captain Kearney in eulogistic terms, while not giving his name in the death list, this Santander had read. The presumption, therefore, was of Kearney being among the survivors.

Thus stood things in the city of Mexico at the time the Mier prisoners entered it, as relates to the persons who have so far found place in our story—Carlos Santander, a colonel on the staff of the Dictator; Don Ignacio Valverde, a Minister of State; his daughter, a reigning belle of society, with no aspirations therefore, but solely on account of her beauty; Florence Kearney, late captain of the Texan *filibusters*, with Cris Rock, guide, scout, and general skirmisher of the same—these last shut up in a loathsome prison, one linked leg to leg with a robber, the other sharing the chain of a murderer, alike crooked in soul as in body!

That for the Texan prisoners there was yet greater degradation in store—one of them, Kearney, was made aware the moment after the gaol-governor had so unceremoniously shut the door of their cell. The teaching of Don Ignacio in New Orleans had not been thrown

away upon him ; and these, with the practice
since accruing through conversation with the
soldiers of their escort, had made him almost a
master of the Spanish tongue.

Carlos Santander either did not think of
this, or supposed the cloister door too thick to
permit of speech in the ordinary tone passing
through it.   It did, notwithstanding; what he
said outside to the governor reaching the
Irishman's ear, and giving him a yet closer
clue to that hitherto enigma—the why he and
Cris Rock had been cast into a common gaol,
among the veriest and vilest of malefactors.

The words of Santander were—

"As you see, Señor Don Pedro, the two
Tejanos are old acquaintances of mine.   I met
them not in Texas, but the United States—
New Orleans—where we had certain relations;
I need not particularize you.   Only to say
that both the gentlemen left me very much in

their debt; and I now wish, above all things, to wipe out the score. I hope I may count upon you to help me?"

There could be no mistaking what he meant. Anything but a repayal of friendly services, in the way of gratitude; instead, an appeal to the gaol-governor to assist him in some scheme of vengeance. So the latter understood it, as evinced by his rejoinder—

"Of course you can, Señor Colonel. Only say what you wish done. Your commands are sufficient authority for me."

"Well," said Santander, after an interval apparently spent in considering. "As a first step, I wish you to give these gentlemen an airing in the street; not alone the Tejanos, but all four."

"*Caspita!*" exclaimed the governor, with a look of feigned surprise. "They ought to be thankful for that."

" They won't, however.   Not likely ; seeing
their company, and the occupation I want
them put at."

" Which is ? "

" A little job in the *zancas!* "

" In which street ? "

" The Calle de Plateros.   I observe that its
stones are up."

" And when ? "

" To-morrow—at midday.   Have them there
before noon, and let them be kept until night,
or, at all events, till the procession has passed.
Do you quite understand me ? "

" I think I do, Señor Colonel.   About their
jewellery—is that to be on ? "

" Every link of it.   I want them to be
coupled, just as they are now—dwarf to giant,
and the two grand gentlemen together."

" *Bueno !*   It shall be done."

So closed the curious dialogue, or, if con--

tinued, what came after it did not reach the ears of Florence Kearney ; they who conversed having sauntered off beyond his hearing. When he had translated what he heard to Cris Rock, the latter, like himself, was uncertain as to what it meant. Not so either of their prison companions, who had likewise listened to the conversation outside—both better comprehending it.

" *Bueno*, indeed ! " cried the dwarf, echoing the gaol-governor's exclamation. " It shall be done. Which means that before this time to-morrow, we'll all four of us be up to our middle in mud. Won't that be nice ? Ha ! ha ! ha ! "

And the imp laughed, as though instead of something repulsive, he expected a pleasure of the most enjoyable kind.

CHAPTER XIV.

ON THE AZOTEA.

IN the city of Mexico the houses are flat roofed, the roof bearing the name of *azotea*. A parapetted wall, some three or four feet in height, runs all round to separate those of the adjacent houses from one another when they chance to be on the same level, and also prevent falling off. Privacy, besides, has to do with this protective screen; the azotea being a piece of almost daily resort, if the weather be fine, and a favourite lounging place, where visitors are frequently received. This peculiarity in dwelling-house architecture has an oriental origin, and is still common among the Moors, as all round the Mediterranean. Strange enough, the Conquistadores found something very similar in the New World —conspicuously among the Mexicans—where the Aztecan houses were flat or terrace topped. Examples yet exist in Northern and New Mexico, in the towns of the Pecos Zuñis, and Moquis. It is but natural, therefore, that the people who now call themselves Mexicans should have followed a pattern thus furnished them by their ancestry in both hemispheres.

Climate has much to do with this sort of roof, as regards its durability; no sharp frosts or heavy snows being there to affect

it.   Besides, in no country in the world
is out-door life more enjoyable than in
Mexico, the rainy months excepted; and
in them the evenings are dry.   Still,
another cause contributes to make the roof
of a Mexican house a pleasant place of
resort.   Sea-coal and its smoke are things
there unknown; indeed chimneys, if not
altogether absent, are few and far between;
such as there are being inconspicuous.   In
the *siempre-verano* (eternal spring) of Anahuac there is no call for them; a wood
fire here and there kindled in some sitting-room being a luxury of a special kind,
indulged in only by the very delicate, or
very rich.   In the kitchens charcoal is the
commodity employed, and as this yields no
visible sign the outside atmosphere is preserved pure and cloudless as that which
overhung the Hesperides.

A well appointed azotea is provided with pots containing shrubs and evergreen plants; some even having small trees, as the orange, lime, camelia, ferns, and palms; while here and there one is conspicuous by a *mirador* (belvedere) arising high above the parapet to afford a better view of the surrounding country.

It would be difficult to find landscape more lovely, or more interesting, than that which surrounds the city of Mexico. Look in what direction one will, the eye is furnished with a feast. Plains, verdant and varied in tint, from the light green of the *milpas* (young maize), to the more sombre *maguey* plants, which, in large plantations (magueyals) occupy a considerable portion of the surface—fields of *chile* pepper and frijoles (kidney beans)—here and there wide sheets of water between,

10

glistening silver-like under the sun—bounding all a periphery of mountains, more than one of their summits white with never-melting snow. The grandest mountains too, since they are the cordilleras of the Sierra Madre or main Andean chain, which here parted by some Plutonic caprice, in its embrace the beautiful valley of Mexico, elevated more than seven thousand feet above the level of the sea.

Surveying it from any roof in the city itself, the scene is one to delight the eye and gladden the heart. And yet on the azotea of a certain house or rather in the *mirador* above it, stood a young lady, who looked over it without delight in her eye or gladness in her heart. Instead, the impression upon her countenance told of thoughts that besides being sad, dwelt not on the landscape or its beauties.

Luisa Valverde it was, thinking of another land, beautiful too, where she had passed several years in exile; the last of them marked by an era the sweetest and happiest of her life. For it was there she first loved; Florence Kearney being he who had won her heart. And the beloved one—where was he now? She knew not; did not even know whether he still lived. He had parted from her without giving any clue, though it gave pain to her— ignorant of the exigencies which had ruled his sudden departure from New Orleans. He had told her, however, of his becoming captain of the volunteer band; which, as she soon after became aware, had proceeded direct to Texas. Furthermore, she had heard all about the issue of the ill-fated expedition; of the gallant struggle made by the men composing it, with the

havoc caused in their ranks; of the survivors being brought on to the city of
Mexico and the cruel treatment they had
been submitted to on the march; of their
daring attempt to escape from the guards,
its successful issue for a time, till their
sufferings among the mountains compelled
them to a second surrender—in short
everything that had happened to that
brave band of which her lover was one
of the leaders.

She had been in Mexico throughout all
this; for shortly after the departure of the
volunteers for Orleans, her father had received the pardon we have spoken of.
And there she had been watching the
Mier Expedition through every step of its
progress, eagerly collecting every scrap of
information relating to it published in the
Mexican papers; with anxious heart, strain-

ing her ears over the lists of killed and wounded. And when at length the account came of the shootings at El Salado, apprehensively as ever scanned she that death-roll of nigh twenty names—the *decimated;* not breathing freely until she had reached the last, and saw that no more among these was his she feared to find.

So far her researches were, in a sense, satisfactory. Still she was not satisfied. Neither to read or hear word of him—that seemed strange; was so in her way of thinking. Such a hero as he, how could his name be hidden? Gallant deeds were done by the Tejanos, their Mexican enemies admitting it. Surely in these Don Florencio had taken part, and borne himself bravely? Yes, she was sure of that. But why had he not been mentioned? And where was he now?

The last question was that which most
frequently occupied her mind, constantly
recurring. She could think of but one
answer to it ; this saddening enough. He
might never have reached the Rio Grande,
but perished on the way. Perhaps his
life had come to an inglorious though not
ignominous end—by disease, accident, or
other fatality—and his body . might now be
lying in some lonely spot of the prairies
where his marching comrades had hastily
buried it.

More than once had Luisa Valverde given
way to such a train of reflection during
the months after her return to Mexico.
They had brought pallor to her cheeks and
melancholy into her heart. So much, that
not all the honours to which her father
had been restored—not all the compliments
paid to herself, nor the Court gaieties in

which she was expected to take part—
could win her from a gloom that seemed
likely to become settled on her soul.

CHAPTER XV.

WAITING AND WATCHING.

AS a rule, people of melancholy temperament, or with a sorrow at the heart, give way to it within doors, in the privacy of their own apartments. The daughter of Don Ignacio had been more often taught to assuage hers upon the house-top, to which she was accustomed to ascend daily, staying there for hours alone. For this she had opportunity; her father busied with State affairs spending most of his time—at least during the diurnal hours—at Government head-quarters in the *Palacio*.

On this day, however, Luisa Valverde mounted up to the azotea with feelings, and under an impulse, very different from that hitherto actuating her. Her behaviour, too, was different. When she made her way up and took stand inside the *Mira-dor*, her eyes instead of wandering all around, or resting dreamily on the land-scape, with no care for its attractions, were turned in a particular direction, and became fixed upon a single point. This was where the road, running from the city to Tacubaya, alongside the aqueduct of Chap-ultepec, parts from the latter, diverging abruptly to the left. Beyond this point the causeway, carried on among maguey

plants, and Peruvian pepper trees, cannot
be seen from the highest house-top in
the city.

Why on this day, more than any other,
did the young lady direct her glance to
the bend in the road, there keeping it
steadfast? For what reason was the expression upon her countenance so different
from that of other days? No listless look
now; instead an earnest eager gaze as
though she expected to see some one,
whose advent was of the greatest interest
to her. It could only be the coming of
some one, as one going would have been
long since visible by the side of the aqueduct.

And one she did expect to come that
way; no grand cavalier on prancing steed,
but a simple pedestrian—in short, her own
servant. She had sent him on an errand

to Tacubaya, and was now watching for, and awaiting his return. It was the nature of his errand which caused her to look for him so earnestly.

On no common business had he been despatched, but one of a confidental character, and required tact in its execution. But Jose, a *mestizo* whom she had commissioned, possessed this, besides having her confidence, and she had no fear of his betraying her. Not that it was a life or death matter; only a question of delicacy. For his errand was to enquire, whether among the Texan prisoners taken to Tacubaya one was called Florence Kearney.

As it was now the third day after their arrival in Mexico, it may be wondered why the young lady had not sought this information before. The explanation is easy.

Her father owned a country house in the environs of San Augustine, some ten miles from the city; and there staying she had only the day before heard that the captive train, long looked for, had at length arrived. Soon as hearing it, she had hastened her return to town, and was now taking steps to ascertain whether her lover still lived.

She did not think of making inquiry at the Accordada, though a rumour had reached her that some of the prisoners were there. But surely not Don Florencio! If alive, it was not likely he would be thus disgraced: at least she could not believe it. Little dreamt she of the malice that was moving, and in secret, to degrade in her eyes the man who was uppermost in her thoughts.

And as little suspected she when one

of the house domestics came upon the
azotea and handed her a large ornamental
envelope, bearing the State arms, that it
was part of the malignant scheme.

Breaking it open she drew out an
embossed and gilded card—a ticket. It
came from the Dictator, inviting Doña
Luisa Valverde to be present in a grand
procession, which was to take place on the
following day; intimating, moreover, that
one of the State carriages would be at
the disposal of herself and party.

There were but few ladies in the city
of Mexico who would not have been
flattered by such an invitation; all the
more from the card bearing the name,
Antonio Lopez de Santa Anna, signed by
himself, with the added phrase "con estima
particular".

But little cared she for the flattery.

Rather did it cause her a feeling of dis-
gust; with something akin to fear. It
was not the first time for the ruler of
Mexico to pay compliments and thus press
his attentions upon her.

Soon as glancing over, she let the des-
pised thing fall, almost flinging it at her
feet; and once more bent her eyes upon
the Tacubaya road, first carrying her glance
along the side of the aqueduct to assure
herself that her messenger had not in the
meanwhile rounded the corner.

He had not, and she continued to watch
impatiently; the invitation to a ride in
the State carriage being as much out of
her mind as though she had never received it.

Not many minutes longer before being
intruded on. This time, however, by no
domestic; instead a lady—like herself,

young and beautiful, but beauty of an
altogether different style. Though of pure
Spanish descent, Lusia Valverde was a
güera; her complexion bright, with hair
of sunny hue. Such there are in Mexico,
tracing their ancestry to the shores of
Biscay's famous bay.

She who now appeared upon the azotea
was dark; her skin showing a tinge of
golden brown, with a profusion of black
hair plaited and coiled as a coronet around
her head. A crayon-like shading showed
upon her upper lip—which on that of a
man would have been termed a moustache—
rendering whiter by contrast teeth already
of dazzling whiteness; while for the same
reason, the red upon her cheeks was of
the deep tint of a damask rose. The
tones of all, however, were in perfect har-
mony; and distributed over features of the

finest mould produced a face in which soft feminine beauty vied with a sort of savage picturesqueness, making it piquantly attractive.

It was altogether a rare bewitching face; part of its witchery being due to the *raza Andalusiana*—and beyond that the Moriscan—but as much of it coming from the ancient blood of Anahuæ—possibly from the famed Malinche herself. For the young lady delineated was the Condesa Almonté —descended from one of *conquistadors* who had wedded an Aztec princess—the beautiful Ysabel Almonté, whose charms were at this time the toast of every *cercle* in Mexico.

Chapter XVI.

A MUTUAL MISAPPREHENSION.

UISA Valverde and Ysabel Almonté were fast friends—so fondly intimate that scarcely a day passed without their seeing one another and exchanging confidences. They lived in the same street; the Condesa having a house of her own, though nominally owned by her grandaunt and guardian. For, besides being beautiful and possessed of a title—

one of the few still found in Mexico,
relics of the old *régime*—Ysabel Almonté
was immensely rich; had houses in the
city, *haciendas* in the country, property
everywhere.   She had a will of her own
as well, and spent her wealth according
to her inclinations, which were all on the
side of generosity, even to caprice.   By
nature a light-hearted, joyous creature, gay
and merry, as one of the bright birds of her
country, it was a rare thing to see sadness
upon her face.   And yet Luisa Valverde,
looking down from the mirador, saw that
now.   There was a troubled expression
upon it, excitement in her eyes, attitude
and gestures, while her bosom rose and
fell in quick pulsations.   True, she had
run up the *escalera*—a stair of four flights—
without pause or rest; and that might
account for her laboured breathing.   But

not for the flush on her cheek, and the sparkle in her eyes. These came from a different cause, though the same one which had carried her up the long stairway without pausing to take breath.

She had not enough now left to declare it; but stood panting and speechless.

"*Madre de Dios!*" exclaimed her friend in an accent of alarm. "What is it, Ysabel?"

"*Madre de Dios!* I say too," gasped the Condesa. "Oh, Luisita! what do you think?"

"What?"

"They've taken him—they have him in prison!"

"He lives then—still lives! Blessed be the Virgin!"

Saying which Luisa Valverde crossed her

arms over her breast, and with eyes raised devotionally towards Heaven, seemed to offer up a mute, but fervent thanksgiving.

" Still lives ! " echoed the Condesa, with a look of mingled surprise and perplexity.

" Of course he does; surely you did not think he was dead ! "

" Indeed I knew not what to think—so long since I saw or heard of him. Oh, I'm so glad he's here, even though in a prison; for while there's life there's hope."

By this the Condesa had recovered breath though not composure of countenance. Its expression alone was changed, from the look of trouble to one of blank astonishment. What could her friend mean? Why glad of his being in a prison? For all the while she was thinking of a *him*.

" Hope ! " she ejaculated again as an echo, then remaining silent, and looking dazed-like.

" Yes, Ysabel ; I had almost despaired of him. But are you sure they have him here in prison. I was in fear that he had been killed in battle, or died upon the march, somewhere in those great prairies of Texas——"

" *Carramba !* " interrupted the young Countess, who, free of speech, was accustomed to interlading it with her country forms of exclamation.

" What's all this about prairies and Texas ? So far as I know, Ruperto was never there in his life."

" Ruperto ! " echoed the other, as the joy which had so suddenly lit up her features as suddenly returning to shadow. " I thought you were speaking of Florencio."

They understood each other now.   Long
since had their love secrets been mutually
confessed ; and Luisa Valverde needed no
telling who Ruperto was.   Independent of
what she had lately learned from the
Condesa, she knew him to be a gentleman of good family, a soldier of some
reputation ; but who—as once her own
father—had the misfortune to belong to
the party now out of power ; many of
them in exile, or retired upon their estates
in the country—for the time taking no
part in politics.   As for himself, he had
not been lately seen in the city of Mexico,
though it was said he was still in the
country ; as rumour had it, hiding away
somewhere among the mountains.   And
rumour went further, even to the defil-
ing of his fair name.   There were reports of
his having become a robber, and that,

under another name he was now chief of a band of *salteadores,* whose deeds were oft heard of on the Acapulco Road, where this crosses the mountains near that place of many murders—the Cruzdel Marques.

Nothing of this sinister tale, however, had reached the ears of Don Ignacio's daughter. Nor till that day—indeed that very hour—had she, more interested in him, heard aught of it. Hence much of the wild excitement under which she was labouring.

"Forgive me, Ysabel!" said her friend, opening her arms, and receiving the Countess in sympathetic embrace, "forgive me for the mistake I have made."

"Nay, 'tis I who should ask forgiveness," returned the other, seeing the misapprehension her words had caused, with their distressing effect. "I ought to have

spoken plainer. But you know how much
my thoughts have been dwelling on dear
Ruperto."

She did know, or should, judging by
herself, and how hers had been dwelling
on dear Florencio.

"But, Ysabel: you say they made him
a prisoner! Who has done that and
why?"

"The soldiers of the State. As to
why, you can easily guess. Because he
belongs to the party of Liberals. That's
why and nothing else. But they don't
say so. I've something more to tell you.
Would you believe it, Luisita, that they
accuse him of being a *salteador?*"

"I can believe him accused of it—some
of those in power now are wicked enough
for anything—but not guilty. You remember we were acquainted with Don

Ruperto, before that sad time when we were compelled to leave the country. I should say he would be the last man to stain his character by becoming a robber."

" The very last man! Robber indeed! My noble Ruperto the purest of patriots, purer than any in this degenerate land. *Ay-de-mi!* "

" Where did they take him and when?"

" Somewhere near San Augustin, and I think, several days ago, though I've only just heard of it."

"Strange that. As you know, I've been staying at San Augustin for the last week or more; and there was no word of such a thing there."

" Not likely there would be; it was all done quietly. Don Ruperto has been living out that way up in the mountains, hiding, if you choose to call it. I know

where, but no matter. Too brave to be
cautious, he had come down to San
Augustin. Some one betrayed him, and
going back he was waylaid by the soldiers,
surrounded and made prisoner. There
must have been a whole host of them,
else they'd never have taken him so easily.
I'm sure they wouldn't and couldn't."

"And where is he now, Ysabel?"

"In prison as I've told you."

"But what prison?"

"That's just what I'm longing to know.
All I've yet heard is that he's in a
prison under the accusation of being a
highwayman. *Santissima!*" she added,
angrily stamping her tiny foot on the
tesselated flags. "They who accuse him
shall rue it. He shall be revenged on
them. I'll see justice done him myself.
Ah! that will I, though it costs me all

I'm worth. Only to think—Ruperto a robber! My Ruperto! *Valga me Dios!*"

By this, the two had mounted up into the mirador—the Senorita Valverde having come down to receive her visitor. And there, the first flurry of excitement over, they talked more tranquilly, or at all events more intelligibly of the affairs mutually affecting them. In those there was much similarity, indeed, in many respects a parrallelism. Yet the feelings with which they regarded them were diametrically opposite. One knew that her lover was in prison, and grieved at it; the other hoped her's might be the same, and would have been glad of it!

A strange dissimilitude, of which the reader has the key.

Beyond what she had already said, the Condesa had little more to communicate, and in her turn became the questioner.

"I can understand now, *amiga mia*, why you spoke of Don Florencio. The Tejano prisoners have arrived, and you are thinking he's amongst them? That's so, is it not!"

"Not thinking, but hoping it, Ysabel."

"Have you taken any steps to ascertain?"

"I have."

"In what way?"

"I've sent a messenger to Tacubaya, where I'm told they've been taken."

"Not all. Some of them have been sent elsewhere. One party, I believe, is shut up in the Acordada."

"What? in that fearful place! among those horrid wretches—the worst criminals we have! The Tejans are soldiers—prisoners of war. Surely they do not deserve such treatment?"

"Deserve it or not, some of them are receiving it. That grand gentleman, Colonel Carlos Santander—your friend by the way—told me so."

The mention of Santander's name, but more a connection with the subject spoken of, produced a visible effect on Luisa Valverde. Her cheek seemed to pale, and suddenly flushed red again. Well she remembered, and vividly recalled, the old enmity between him and Don Florencio. Too well, and a circumstance of most sinister recollection as matters stood now. She had thought of it before ; was thinking of it all the time, and therefore the words of the Condesa started no new train of reflection. They but intensified the fear she already felt, for a time holding her speechless.

Not noticing this, and without waiting

a rejoinder, the other ran on, still interrogating :

"Whom have you trusted with this
delicate mission, may I ask?"

"Only José."

"Well; José, from what I've seen of
him, is worthy of the trust. That is so
far as honesty is concerned, and possibly
cleverness. But, *amiga mia*, he's only a
humble servitor, and out there in Tacubaya, among the garrison soldiers, or if it
be in any of the prisons, he may experience a little difficulty in obtaining the
information you seek. Did you give him
any money to make matters easy?"

"He has my purse with him, with
permission to use it as he may see best."

"Ah! then you may safely expect his
bringing back a good account, or at all
events one that will settle the question

you wish to have settled. Your purse should be a key to Don Florencio's prison—if he be inside one anywhere in Mexico."

"Oh! I hope he is."

"Wishing your *amanté* in a prison! That would sound strange enough; if one didn't understand it."

"I'd give anything to know him there—all I have to be assured he still lives."

"Likely enough you'll soon hear. When do you expect your messenger to be back?"

"At any moment. He's been gone many hours ago. I was watching for him when you came up—yonder on the Tacubaya Road. I see nothing of him yet, but he may have passed while we've been talking."

"*Muy amiga mia!* How much our doings this day have been alike. I, too, have despatched a messenger to find out all about Ruperto, and am now awaiting his return. I ran across to tell you of it. And now that we're together let us stay till we know the worst or the best. God help us both; for, to make use of the phrase I've heard among *marineros*, we're 'both in the same boat'. What is this?'" she added, stooping, and taking up the gilded card which had been all the while lying upon the floor. "Oh, indeed! Invitation to an airing in one of the State carriages—with such a pretty compliment appended! How free El Excellentissimo is with his flattery. For myself I detest both him and it. You'll go, won't you?"

"I don't wish it."

"No matter about wishing; I want you. And so will your father, I'm sure."

"But why do you want me?"

"Why, so that you may take me with you."

"I would rather wait till I hear what father says."

"That's all I ask, *amiga*. I shall be contented with his dictum, now feeling sure—"

She was interrupted by the pattering of feet upon the stone stairway; two pairs of them, which told that two individuals were ascending. The heavy tread proclaimed them to be men. Presently their faces showed over the baluster rail, and another step brought them upon the roof. Both ladies regarding them with looks of eager inquiry, glided down out of the mirador to meet them.

For they were the two messengers that had been despatched separately, though on errands so very similar.

12

Returning they had met by the front door, and entered the house together. Each having had orders to deliver his report, and without delay, was now acting in obedience to them.

Two and two they stood upon the azotea, —the men, hat in hand, stood in front of their respective mistresses; not so far apart, but that each mistress might have heard what the servant of the other said; for on their part there was no wish or reason for concealment.

"Senorita," reported José, "the gentleman you sent me to enquire about is not in Tacubaya."

Almost a cry came from Luisa Valverde's lips, as with paled cheek, she said—

"You've not heard of him, then?"

But the colour quickly returned at the answer—

"I have, Senorita; more, I have seen him."

" Seen Don Florencio ! — where ? Speak quick, José ! "

" In the Acordada ! "

" In the Acordada ! " in still another voice— that of the Condesa speaking in a similar tone, as though it were an echo ; for she, too, had just been told that her lover was in the same gaol.

" I saw him in a cell, my lady," continued the Countess's man, now taking precedence. " They had him coupled to another prisoner— a Tejano."

" He was in one of the cells, Senorita," spoke José, also continuing his report, "chained to a robber."

Chapter XVII.

POR LAS ZANCAS!

N all cities there is a street favoured by fashion. This in Mexico is the Calle de Plateros (street of the silversmiths), so called because there the workers in precious metals and dealers in bijouterie "most do congregate".

In this street the *jovenes dorador* (gilded youth) of modern Tenochtitlan strolled in tight-fitting patent leather boots, canary-coloured kid gloves, cane in hand, and quizzing-glass to the eye. There, too, the senoras and senoritas go shopping bareheaded, with but the shawl thrown over the crown hood fashion.

When out only for promenade, none of these linger long in the street of the silversmiths. They but pass through it on their way to the *Alameda*, a sort of half-park, half-garden, devoted to the public use, and tastefully laid out in walks, terraces, and parterres with flowers, and fountains; grand old evergreen trees overshadowing all. For in that summery clime shade, not sun, is the desideratum. Here the *jovenes corados* spent part of the afternoons sauntering along the arcaded walks, or seated around the great fountain watching the play of its crystal waters. But with an eye to something besides—the senoritas, who are there, too, flirting the fans with a dexterity which speaks

of much practice. Speaks of something more.
Not every movement made by these rustling
segments of circles is intended to create
currents of air, and cool the heated skin.
Many a twist and turn, watched with anxious
eyes, conveys intelligence interesting as words
never spoken. In Mexico many a love tale is
told, passion declared, jealous pang caused or
alleviated, by the mute languages of fans and
fingers.

Though the Calle de Plateros terminates at
the gate of the Alameda, the same line of
street is continued half-a-mile further on, to
the fashionable drive of the *Pasco Nuevo*,
sometimes called Pasco de Buccareli, from the
Viceroy who ruled New Spain when it was laid
out. It is the Rotten Row of Mexico, for it is
a ride as well as a drive; and at a certain hour
of the afternoon a stream of carriages, with
strings of horsemen, may be seen tending

towards it, the carriages drawn, some of them by mules, others by the small native horses, and a distinguished few by large English or American animals, there known as *frisones*. It is the top thing to have a pair of "*frisones*".

In the carriages, the senoras and senoritas are seen attired in their richest robes—full evening dress—bare-armed and bare-headed, their hair, usually black, ablaze with jewels or entwined with flowers fresh picked—the sweet-scented suchil, the white star-like jasmine, and crimson grenadine. Alongside ride the cavaliers, in high-peaked, stump-leather saddles, their steeds capering and prancing; each rider, to all appearance, requiring the full strength of his arms to control his mount, while insidiously using his spurs to render the animal uncontrollable. The more it pitches and plunges the better he is pleased, provided

the occupants of the carriages have their
eyes on him.

Every day in the year—except during the
week of *Guaresma* (Lent), when capricious
fashion takes him to the Paseo Viejo, or *Lav
Vigas*, on the opposite side of the city—can
this brilliant procession be seen moving along
the Calle de Plateros, and its continuation, the
Calle de San Francisco.

But in this same thoroughfare one may often
witness a spectacle less resplendent, with
groups aught but gay.   Midway along the
street runs a deep drain or sewer, not as in
European cities permanently covered up, but
loosely flagged over, the flags removable at
will.   This, the *zanca*, is more of a stagnant
sink than a drainage sewer ; since from the
city to the outside country there is scarce an
inch of fall to carry off the sewage.   As a
consequence it accumulates in the zancas till

they are brimming full, and with a stuff
indescribable. Every garbage goes there—all
the refuse of household product is shot into
them. At periodical intervals they are cleared
out, else the city would soon be aflood in its
own filth. It is often very near it, the blue
black liquid seen oozing up between the flag-
stones that bridge over the zancas, filling the
air with a stench intolerable. Ever recurring
revolutions make the municipal authorities of
Mexico careless about their charge and neglect-
ful of their duties. But when the scouring-out
process is going on, the sights are still more
offensive, and the smells too. Then the flags
are lifted and laid on one side—exposing all
the impurity—while the stuff is tossed to the
other, there to lie festering for days, or until
dry enough to be more easily removed. For
all it does not stop the circulation of the
carriages. The grand dames seated in them

pass on, now and then showing a slight con-
tortion in their pretty noses. But they would
not miss their airing in the Paseo were it
twenty times worse—that they wouldn't. To
them, as to many of their English sisterhood
in Hyde Park, the afternoon drive is everything—to some, as report says, even more than
meat or drink; since they deny themselves
these for the keeping of the carriage.

It may be imagined that the scouring-out of
the zancas is a job for which labourers are not
readily obtained. Even the *pelado* turns up
his nose at it, and the poorest proletarian will
only undertake the task when starvation is
staring him in the face. For it is not only
dirty, but deemed degrading. It is, therefore,
one of the travaux-forces which, as a matter of
necessity, falls to the lot of the " gaol-bird ".
Convicts are the scavengers; criminals sen-
tenced to long periods of imprisonment, of

whom there are often enough in the *carceles* of Mexico to clean out all the sewers in the country. Even by these it is a task looked upon with repugnance, and usually assigned to them as a punishment for prison derelictions. Not that they so much regard the dirt or the smells ; it is the toil which offends them—the labour being hard, and often requiring to be done under a hot, broiling sun.

To see them it is a spectacle of a rather curious kind, though repulsive. Coupled two and two—for the precaution is taken, and not unfrequently needed—to keep their leg-chains on ; up in mud to the middle of their bodies, and above bespattered with it—such mud too ! many of them with faces that, even when clean, are aught but nice to look at ; their eyes now flashing fierce defiance, now bent down and sullen, they seemed either at enmity or out of sorts with all mankind. Some among them, however, make light of it, bandy words with the passers-by, jest, laugh, sing, shout, and swear, which to a sensitive mind but makes the spectacle more sad.

All this understood, it may well be conceived with what anxiety Florence Kearney listened to that snatch of dialogue between Santander and the gaol governor outside the cell. He did not even then quite comprehend the nature of what was intended for them. But the sharer of his chain did, who soon after made it all known to him, he passing the knowledge on to Cris Rock. So when, on the next morning, the governor again presented himself at the door of their cell, saying :

" Now gentlemen, get ready to take a little exercise "—they knew what sort of exercise was meant.

He, however, believing them ignorant of it—for he was not aware they had overheard his outdoor speech with Santander, added ironically :

"It's a special favour I'm going to give you—at the request of Senior Colonel Santander, who, as I've seen, takes a friendly interest in some of you. For your health's sake, he has asked me to give you a turn upon the streets ; which I trust you will enjoy and get benefit by."

Don Pedro was a born joker, and felt conceit in his powers as a satirist. In the present instance his irony was shaftless, being understood.

The dwarf was the only one who deigned rejoinder.

"Ha, ha, ha !" he yelled in his wild unearthly way. "Turn *upon* the streets ! That's fine for you, Don Pedro. A turn *under* the streets—that's what you mean, isn't it ? "

He had been long enough in the gaol governor's charge to know the latter's name, and was accustomed to address him thus familiarly. The deformed creature was fearless from his very deformity, which in a way gave him protection.

" *Vayate Zorillo*," returned the Governor, slightly put out and evidently a little nettled, "You're too fond of jesting—or trying. I'll take that out of you, and I mean to give you a lesson in good manners this very day." Then fixing his eyes upon Riras, he added : " Señor Don Ruperto, I should be only too happy to let you off from the little excursion your prison companions are about to make and save you the fatigue. But my orders are rigorous. They come from the highest quarters, and I dare not disobey them."

This was all pure irony, intended but

to torment him; at least so the robber seemed to understand it. For, instead of accepting it in a friendly sense he turned savagely on his tormentor, hissing out :

" I know you daren't disobey them, dog that you are ! Only such as you would be governor of a gaol like this : you, who turned coat and disgraced the sword you wore at Zacatecas. Do your worst, Don Pedro Arias ! I defy you."

" *Cascaras !* how swelling big you talk, Señor Capitan Rivas ! Ah ! well. I'll let a little of the wind out of you too, before you bid good-bye to the Acordada. Even the Condesa, grand dame though she is, won't be able to get you clear of my clutches so easy as you may be thinking. La Garrota is the lady likeliest to do that."

After thus spitefully delivering himself, he called to some prison warders in waiting in the court outside, and commanded them to come up to him.

"Here," he directed, "take these two pairs and hand them over to the guard at the gate. You know what for, Dominquez?" The half interrogatory was addressed to a big, hulking fellow, chief of the turnkeys, who looked all Acordada.

"*Por Cierto, Señor Gobernador,*" he rejoined with a significant look, after giving the prison salute to his superior. "I know all about it."

"See, moreover, that they be kept all day at it; that's my orders."

"Sure will I, Señor," was the compliant rejoinder.

After which the man twitted with turning his coat, turned his back upon the place where he had been so ungraciously received, going off to more agreeable quarters.

"Now, gentlemen!" said the gaoler, stepping up to the door of the cell, "*Por las Zancas!*"

CHAPTER XVIII.

TYRANT AND TOOL.

L Excellentissimo Illustrissimo General Don José Antonio Lopez de Santa Anna.

Such the twice sesquipedalian name and title of him who at this time wielded the destinies of Mexico. For more than a quarter of a century this man had been the curse of the young Republic—its direst, deadliest bane. For although his rule was not continuous, its evil effects were. Unfortunately, the demoralisation brought about by despotism, extends beyond the reign or life of the despot ; and Santa Anna had so debased the Mexican people, both socially and politically, as to render them unfitted for almost any form of constitutional government. They had become incapable of distinguishing between the friends of freedom and its foes ; and in the intervals of Liberal administration, because the Millennium did not immediately show itself, and make all rich, prosperous and happy, they leaped to the conclusion that its failure was due to the existing *régime*, making no account, or allowance, for the still uncicatrised wounds of the body politic being the work of his wicked predecessor.

This ignorance of political cause and effect is alas ! not alone confined to Mexico. There

is enough of it in England, too—as in every
other nation. But in the earlier days of
the Mexican Republic the baneful weed
flourished with unusual vigour and rankness
—to the benefit of Antonio Lopez de Santa
Anna, and the blight of his country. De-
posed and banished so many times that
their number is not easily remembered, he
was ever brought back again—to the wonder
of people then, and the puzzle of historians
yet. The explanation, however, is simple
enough. He reigned through corruption
that he had himself been instrumental in
creating; through militarism and an abomin-
able *Chauvinism*—this last as effective an
instrument as the oppressor can wield.
Divide et impera is a maxim of despotic
state-craft, old as depotism itself; "flatter
and rule" is a method equally sure, and
such Santa Anna practised to its full. He

let pass no opportunity of flattering the
national vanity, which brought the Mexican
nation to shame, with much humiliation—
as the French at a later period, and as it
must every people that aims at no higher
standard of honour than what may be de-
rived from self-adulation.

At the time I am writing of, the chief
of the Mexican Republic was aiming at
" Imperium "—eagerly straining for it. Its
substance he already had, the " Libertas "
having been long since eliminated from his
system of government, and trodden under
foot. But the title he had not acquired yet.
He yearned to wear the purple, and be
styled " Imperador," and in order to prepare his subjects for the change, already
kept a sort of Imperial court, surrounding
it with grand ceremonials. As a matter of
course, these partook of a military character ;

being himself not only political head of the
State, but commander-in-chief of its armies.
As a consequence *Palacio*, his official residence, was beset with soldier guards, officers
in gorgeous uniforms loitering about the
gates or going out and in, and in the Plazza
Grande at all times exhibiting the spectacle
of a venerable Champ de Mars. No one
passing through the Mexican metropolis at
this period would have supposed it the chief
city of a Republic.

On that same day, in which Carlos Santander had shown himself at the Acordada,
only at an early hour, the would-be Emperor
was seated in his apartment of the palace
in which he was wont to give audience to
ordinary visitors. He had got through the
business affairs of the morning, dismissed his
Ministers, and was alone when one of the
aides-de-camp in attendance entered with

a card, and respectfully saluting him, laid it on the table before him.

"Yes ; say I can see him. Tell him to come in," he directed, soon as reading the name on the card.

In the door on its second opening appeared Carlos Santander, in the uniform of a colonel of Hussars, gold bedizened and laced from collar to cuffs.

"Ah ! Señor Don Carlos !" exclaimed the Dictator in a joyous, jocular way ; " What's your affair ? Coming to tell me of some fresh conquest you've made among the *muchachas?* From your cheerful countenance I should say it's that."

" Excellentissimo ! "

" Oh ! you needn't deny, or look so demure about it. Well, you're a lucky fellow to be the lady killer I've heard say you are."

" Your Excellency, that's only say-say ;

I ought rather to call it slander. I've no
ambition to be thought such a character.
Quite the reverse, I assure you."

" If you could assure me ; but you can't.
I've had you long enough under my eye
to know better. Haven't I observed your
little flirtations with quite half-a-score of
our senoritas ; among them a very charming
young lady you met in Lousiana, if I mistake not."

Saying this, he fixed his eyes on Santander's
face in a searching interrogative way, as
though he himself felt more than a common
interest in the charming young lady who
had been met in Lousiana.

Avoiding his glance, as evading the question, the other rejoined—

" It is very good of your Excellency to take
such interest.in me, and I'm grateful. But I
protest—

"Come, come! *amigo mio!* No protesta-
tions. 'Twould only be adding perjury to
profligacy. Ha! ha! ha!"

And the grand dignitary leaned back in his
chair, laughing. For it was but badinage,
and he in no way intended lecturing the staff-
colonel on his morality, nor rebuking him for
any backslidings. Instead, what came after
could but encourage him in such wise, his
chief continuing—

" Yes, Señor Don Carlos, I'm aware of your
amourettes, for which I'm not the man to be
hard upon you. In that regard, I myself get
the credit—so rumour says—of living in a
glass house, so I cannot safely throw stones.
Ha! ha!"

The tone of his laugh, with his self-satisfied
look, told of his being aught but angry with
rumour for so representing him.

" Well, Excellentissimo," here put in the

subordinate ; "it don't much signify what the world says, so long as one's conscience is clear."

"*Bravo-bravissimo!*" exclaimed the Most Excellent. "Ha-ha-ha!" he continued, in still louder cachination. "Carlos Santander turned moralist! And moralizing to me! It's enough to make a horse laugh. Ha-ha-ha!"

The staff-colonel appeared somewhat disconcerted, not knowing what all this might be tending to. However, he ventured to remark :

"I am glad to find your Excellency in such good humour this morning."

"Ah! that's because you've come to ask some favour from me, I suppose." Santa Anna had a habit of interlarding his most familiar and friendly discourse with a little satire, sometimes very disagreeable to those he conversed with. "But never mind," he rattled on, "though I confess some surprise at your hypocrisy, which is all thrown away upon me, *amigo!* I don't at all wonder at your success with the signoritas. You're a handsome fellow, Don Carlos ; and if it weren't for that scar on your cheek——By the way, you never told me how you came by it. You hadn't it when you were last with us."

The red flushed into Santander's face, and up over his forehead to the roots of his hair. He had told no one in Mexico, nor anywhere else, how he came by that ugly thing on his jaw, which beard could not conceal, and which he felt as a brand of Cain.

"It's a scar of a sword cut, your Excellency. I got it in a duel."

"Ah! An honourable wound, then. But where ?"

"In New Orleans."

"Just the place for that sort of thing, as I know, having been there myself." (Santa

Anna had made a tour of the States, on
parole, after the battle of San Jacinto,
where he was taken prisoner.) "A very den
of duellists is Nuevo Orleans ; many of them
maitres d'escrime. But who was your antagonist ? I hope you gave him as good as you
got."

"I did, your Excellency ; that, and more."

"You killed him ?"

"Not quite. I would have done so, but
that my second interposed, and persuaded me
to let him off."

"Well ; he hasn't let you off, anyhow.
What was the quarrel about ? *Carrai!* I
needn't ask ; the old, orthodox cause—a lady,
of course ? "

"Nay ; for once your Excellency is in error.
Our *desajio* originated in something quite
different."

"What thing ?"

" An endeavour on my part to do a service to Mexico and its honoured ruler."

" Oh, indeed! In what way, Señor Colonel?"

" That band of *filibusteros*, of which, as your Excellency will remember——"

" Yes—yes," interrupted Santa Anna impatiently. He evidently knew all about that, and preferred hearing no more of it. " It was one of the *filibusteros* you fought with, I suppose ? "

" Yes, Excellentissimo ; the one they chose for their captain."

" You were angry at his being preferred to yourself, and so called him out ? Well ; that was cause enough to a man of your mettle. But what became of him afterwards ? Was he among those at Mier ? "

" He was."

" Killed there ? "

" No, your Excellency; only taken prisoner."

" Shot at Solado ? "

" Neither that, Excellentissimo."

" Then he must be here ? "

" He is here, your Excellency."

" What's his name ? "

" Kearney—Florence Kearney, *un Irlandes.*"

A peculiar expression came over Santa Anna's features, a sort of knowing look, as much as to say the name was not new to him. Nor was it. That very morning, only an hour before, Don Ignacio Valverde had audience of him on a matter relating to this same man— Florence Kearney; in short, to obtain clemency for the young Irishman—full pardon, if possible. But the Minister had been dismissed with only vague promises. His influence at court was still not very great, and about the motive for his application—as also who it originated from—Santa Anna had conceived suspicions.

Of all this he said nothing to the man before him now, simply inquiring:

" Is the *Irlandes* at Tacubaya ? "

" No, your Excellency ; he's in the Acordada."

" Since you had the disposal of the Tejano prisoners, I can understand that," returned the Dictator with a significant shrug. " It's about him, then, you're here, I suppose. Well, what do you want ? "

" Your authority, Excellentissimo, to punish him as he deserves."

" For making that tracing on your cheek, eh ? You repent not having punished him more at the time when you yourself had the power ? Isn't it so, Señor Colonel ? "

Santander's face reddened, as he made reply:

" Not altogether, your Excellency. There's something besides, for which he deserves to be treated differently from the others."

Santa Anna could have given a close guess at what the exceptional something was. To his subtle perception a little love drama was gradually being disclosed; but he kept his thoughts to himself, with his eyes still searchingly fixed on Santander's face.

"This Kearney," continued the latter, "though an Irishman, is one of Mexico's bitterest enemies, and especially bitter against your Excellency. In a speech he made to the *filibusteros*, he called you an usurper, tyrant, traitor to liberty and your country—aye, even coward. Pardon me for repeating the vile epithets he made use of."

Santa Anna's eyes now scintillated with a lurid sinister light, as if filled with fire, ready to blaze out. In the American newspapers he had often seen his name coupled with such opprobrious phrases, but never without feeling savagely wrathful. And not the less that his own innate consciousness told him it was all as said.

" *Chingara !* " he hissed out, for he was not above using this vulgar exclamation. " If it is true what you say, Don Carlos, as I presume it is, you can do as you like with this dog of an *Irlandes!* have him shot, or have him despatched by *La Garrotta,* which ever seems best to you. But no—stay ! That won't do yet. There's a question about these Tejenos with the United States Minister ; and as this Kearney is an Irishman, and so a British subject, the representative of that country may make trouble too. So till all this is settled the *Irlandes* musn't be either shot or gar-rotted. Instead, let him be treated tenderly. You comprehend ? "

The staff-colonel did comprehend ; the emphasis on the " tenderly " made it impossible for him to mistake the Dictator's meaning,

14

which was just as he desired it. As he passed
out of the presence, and from the room, his
countenance was lit up, or rather darkened,
by an expression of fiendish triumph. He
now had it in his power to humiliate them
who had so humbled him.

"Quite a little comedy!" soliloquised Santa
Anna, as the door closed on his subordinate.
"In which, before it's played out, I may
myself take a part. She's a charming creature
this Senorita Valverde. But, ah! nothing to
the Condesa. That woman—witch, devil, or
whatever I may call her—bids fair to do what
woman never did—make a fool of Lopez de
Santa Anna."

CHAPTER XIX.

A WOODEN-LEGGED LOTHARIO.

OR some time the Dictator remained in his seat lighting cigarrito
after cigarrito, and puffing away
at them furiously. The look of light frivolity
had forsaken his face, which was now over-
cast with gloom.

At this time, as said, he wielded supreme
unlimited power over the Mexican people
—even to life and death. For although

he might not recklessly or openly decree this, he could bring it about secretly—by means which if rumour spoke true, he had more than once made use of. Indeed, there stood against his name more than one well-confirmed record of assassination.

Thought of this may have had something to do with the cloud that had come over his features; though not for any qualms of conscience for the murders he may have committed or hired others to commit. More likely a fear that he himself might some day meet a similar fate; like all despots he dreaded the steel of the assassin. By his corrupt administration, he had encouraged bravoism till it had become a dangerous element in the social life of his country— almost an institution—and was but natural he should fear the bravo's blade turned against himself.

Another apprehension may at this time have been troubling him. Although to all appearance secure in the dictatorial chair, with a likelihood of his soon converting it into a real throne, he had his misgivings about this security. By imprisonments, executions, banishments, and confiscations, he had done all in his power to annihilate the liberal party. But though crushed and feeble now, its strength was but in abeyance, its spirit still lived, and might again successfully assert itself. No man knew this better than he himself; and no better teacher could he have had than his own life's history, with its alternating chapters of triumph and defeat. Even then there was report of a *pronunciamento* in one of the northern cities of the Republic—the State, by a polite euphemism, being still so designated. Only a faint " gritto " it was, but with a tone that resembled the rumbling of distant thunder, which might yet be heard louder and nearer.

Little, however, of matters either revolutionary or political was he thinking now. The subject uppermost in his mind was that latent on his lips—woman. Not in a general way, but with thoughts specially bent upon one of them, or both, with whose names he had just been making free. As his soliloquy told, a certain "Condesa" had first place in his reflections, she being no other than the Condesa Almonté. In his wicked way he had made love to this young lady, as to many others; but, unlike as with many others, he had met repulse. Firm, though without indignation, his advances not yet having gone so far, nor been so bold, as to call for this. He had only commenced skirmishing with her; a preliminary stroke of his tactics being that in-

vitation to ride in the State carriage extended
to Dona Luisita Valverde, while withheld
from the Countess—an astute manœuvre on
his part and, as he supposed, likely to serve
him. In short, the old sinner was playing
the old game of "piques". Nor did he think
himself so ancient as to despair of winning
at it. In such contests he had too often
come off victorious, and success might attend
upon him still. Vain was he of his personal
appearance, and in his earlier days not without some show of reason. In his youth
Santa Anna would claim to be called, if
not handsome, a fairly good-looking man.
Though a native Mexican, a *Vera-cruzano*,
he was of pure Spanish race and good blood
—the boasted *sangre azul*. His features
were well formed, oval, and slightly aquiline,
his complexion dark, yet clear, his hair and
moustaches black, lustrous, and profuse. But

for a sinster cast in his eyes not always
observable, his countenance would have been
pleasing enough. As it was he prided himself upon it even now that he was well up
in years, and his hair becoming silvered.
As for the moustaches, black pomatum kept
them to their original colour.

One thing soured him, even more than
advancing age—his wooden leg. 'Tis said
he could never contemplate that without an
expression of pain coming over his features,
as though there was gout in the leg itself
giving him a twinge. And many the time
—nay hundreds of times—did he curse Prince
de Joinville. For it was in defending Vera
Cruz against the French, commanded by the
latter, he had received the wound, which
rendered amputation of the limb necessary.
In a way he ought to have blessed the Prince,
and been grateful for the losing of it rather

than otherwise. Afterwards the mishap stood him in good stead; at election times when he was candidate for the Chief Magistracy of the State. Then he was proud to parade the artificial limb; and did so to some purpose. It was indeed, an important element in his popularity, and more than once proved an effective aid to his reinstatement.

With a grim look, however, he regarded it now. For though it had helped him politically, he was not thinking of politics, and in what he was thinking about he knew it an obstruction. A woman to love a man with a wooden leg! And such a woman as Ysabel Almonté! Not that he put it to himself in that way; far from it. He had still too good an opinion, if not of his personal appearance, at least of his powers otherwise, and he even then felt confident of success. For he had just succeeded in removing

another obstacle which seemed likely to be
more in his way than the wooden leg. He
had but late come to know of it; but as
soon as knowing, had taken measures to avert
the danger dreaded—by causing the imprisonment of a man. For it was a man he feared,
or suspected, as his competitor for the affections of the Condesa. It had cost him no
small trouble to effect this individual's arrest,
or rather capture. He was one of the pre-
scribed, and in hiding; though heard of
now and then as being at the head of the
band of *salteadore*—believed to have turned
highwayman.

But he had been taken at length, and
was at that moment in the gaol of the
Acordada; which Santa Anna well knew,
having himself ordered his incarceration there,
and given other instructions regarding him to
the gaol governor, who was one of his creatures.

After sitting for some time, as he stretched out his hand, and held the end of his paper cigar to the red coals burning in a *brazere* on the table before him, the frown upon his features changed to a demoniac smile. Possibly from the knowledge that this man was now in his power. Sure was he of this; but what would he not have given to be as sure of her being so too !

Whether his reflections were sweet or bitter, or which predominated, he was not permitted longer to indulge in them. The door again opening—after a tap asking permission to enter—showed the same aide-de-camp. And on a similar errand as before, differing only in that now he placed two cards on the table instead of one ; the cards themselves being somewhat dissimilar to that he had already brought in.

And with altogether a different air did

Santa Anna take them up for examination. He was enough interested at seeing by their size and shape, that those now desiring an audience of him were ladies. But on reading the names, his interest rose to agitation; such as the aide-de-camp never before had seen him exhibit, and which so much astonished the young officer that he stood staring wonderingly, if not rudely, at the grand dignitary, his chief. His behaviour, however, was not noticed, the Dictator's eyes being all upon the cards. Only for an instant though. If he gave ready reception to his late visitor, still readier did he seem desirous of according to those now seeking speech with him.

"Conduct the ladies in," was his almost instantaneous command, as quickly retracted. For soon as spoken he countermanded it; seemingly from some after thought which, as a codicil, had suddenly occurred to him.

Then followed a chapter of instructions to the aide-de-camp, confidential, and to the effect that the ladies were not to be immediately introduced. He was to keep them in conversation in the anti-chamber outside, till he should hear the bell.

Judging by his looks as he went out the young subaltern was more than satisfied with the delay thus enjoined upon him. It was aught but a disagreeable duty; for, whether acquainted with the ladies who were in waiting, or not, he must have seen that both were bewitchingly beautiful—one being Luisa Valverde, the other Ysabel Almonté.

Chapter XX.

A PAIR OF BEAUTIFUL PETITIONERS.

OON as the aide-de-camp had closed the door behind him, Santa Anna sprang up from his seat and hastily stumped it to a large cheval glass which stood on one side of the room. Squaring himself before this he took survey of his person from crown to toes. He gave a pull or two at his moustaches, twisting their points, and turning them upward along his cheeks. Then running his fingers comb-like, through his hair, he gave that also a jaunty set. In fine, straightening himself in his gold-braided uniform frock, with a last glance down to his feet—this resulting in a slight grimace—he returned to the state chair and reseated himself.

With all his gallantry and politeness— and to these he made much pretension—it was not his custom to receive lady visitors standing. In the upright attitude the artificial leg made him look stiff, and he preferred stowing it away under the table. Besides, there was his dignity, as the grand figure-head of the nation, which he now wished to have its full effect. Leaning forward, he gave a downward blow to the spring of the table bell; then assuming an attitude of expectant grandeur, sate expectant.

This time the aide-de-camp required no passing to and fro; and the door again opening, the ladies were ushered into the august presence.

In their air and manner they betrayed agitation too, while the serious expression upon their features told they were there on no trivial errand.

"Pray be seated, ladies," said the Dictator, after exchanging salutations with them. "'Tis not often the Condesa Almonté honours the Palacio with her presence, and for the Senorita Valverde, were it not for official relations with her father, I fear we should see even less of her than we do."

While speaking he pointed to a couple of couch chairs that stood near the table.

They sat down rather hesitatingly, and slightly trembling. Not that either would

have been at all timid had the occasion
been a common one. Both were of Mexico's best blood, the Condesa one of the
old *noblesse* who hold their heads higher
even than the political chief of the state,
when he chances to be—as more than
once has occurred—an adventurer of hum-
bler birth. Therefore, it was not any awe
of the great dignitary that now unnerved
them, but the purpose for which they
were seeking speech with him. Whether
Santa Anna guessed it, or not, could not
be told by his looks. An experienced
diplomatist, he could keep his features fixed
and immovable as the Sphinx, or play
them to suit the time and the tune. So,
after having delivered himself, as above,
with the blandest of smiles upon his face,
he remained silent, awaiting the rejoinder.

It was the Condesa who made it.

15

"Your Excellency," she said, doing her utmost to look humble; "we have come to beg a favour from you."

A gratified look, like a gleam of light, illuminated Santa Anna's swarthy features. Ysabel Almonté begging favours from him! What better could he have wished? With all his command of features he but ill concealed the triumph he now felt. It flashed up in his eyes, as he said respondingly,

"A favour you would ask? Well, if it be within my power to grant it, neither the Condesa Almonté, nor the Doña Luisa Valverde need fear refusal. Be frank, then, and tell me what it is."

The Countess, with all her courage, still hesitated to declare it. For despite the ready promise of compliance, she did fear a refusal; since it had been asked for that same morning and though not absolutely refused, the answer left but little hope of its being conceded.

As is known, at an earlier hour Don Ignacio had paid a visit to the Palacio, to seek clemency for a prisoner-of-war, Florence Kearney. But pardon for a state prisoner was also included in his application—that being Ruperto Rivas. Of all this the ladies were well aware, since it was at their instigation, and through their importunity he had acted. It was only, therefore, by the urgency of a despairing effort, as a *dernier ressort*, these had now sought the presence as petitioners, and naturally they dreaded denial.

Noting the Condesa's backwardness—a thing, new but not displeasing to him, since it gave promise of influence over her—Santa Anna said interrogatively :

"Might this favour, as you are pleased to term it, have aught to do with a request lately made to me by Don Ignacio Valverde ?"

" 'Tis the same, your Excellency," answered
the Countess at length recovering spirit, but
still keeping up the air of meek supplication
she had assumed.

" Indeed !" exclaimed the Dictator, adding,
" that grieves me very much."

He made an attempt to look sorry ; though
it needed none for him to appear chagrined.
This he was in reality, and for reasons intelli-
gible.   Here were two ladies both of whom he
had amatory designs upon, each proclaiming
by her presence—as it were telling him to his
teeth, the great interest she felt in another—
that or she would not have been there !

" But why, Excellentissimo ?" asked the
Countess, entreatingly.   " What is there to
grieve you in giving their freedom to two men
—gentlemen, neither of whom has been guilty
of crime, and who are in prison only for offences
your Excellency can easily pardon ? "

" Not so easily as you think, Condesa. You forget that I am but official head of the State, and have others to consult—my Ministers and the Congress—in affairs of such magnitude. Know, too, that both these men for whom you solicit pardon have been guilty of the gravest offences ; one of them a foreigner, an enemy of our country, taken in arms against it ; the other, I am sorry to say, a citizen, who has become a rebel, and worse still, a robber !"

" 'Tis false !" exclaimed the Countess, all at once changing tone, and seeming to forget the place she was in and the presence.   " Don Ruperto Rivas is no robber ; never was, nor rebel either ; instead the purest of patriots ! "

Never looked Ysabel Almonté lovelier than at that moment—perhaps never woman. Her spirit roused, cheeks red, eyes sparkling with indignation, attitude erect — for she had started up from her chair—she seemed to be the very impersonation of defiance, angry, but beautiful. No longer meek or supplicating now. Instinct or intuition told her it would be of no use pleading further, and she had made up her mind for the worst.

The traits of beauty which her excitement called forth, added piquancy to her natural charms, and inflamed Santa Anna's wicked passions all the more. But more than any of them revenge. For now he knew how much the fair petitioner was interested in the man whose suit she had preferred. With a cold cynicism—which, however, cost him an effort—he rejoined:

"That, perhaps, is your way of thinking, Condesa. But it remains to be proved—and the prisoner you speak of shall have an opportunity of proving it—with his innocence in every respect. That much I can promise you. The same for him," he added, turning to Luisa Valverde, "in whom, if I mistake not, the Dona Luisa is more especially interested. These *gentlemen* prisoners shall have a fair trial, and justice done them. Now, ladies! can you ask more of me?"

They did not; both seeing it would be to no purpose. Equally purposeless to prolong the interview; and they turned toward the door, the daughter of Don Ignacio, leading where she had before followed.

This was just as Santa Anna wished it. Seemingly forgetting of his cork leg, and the limp he took such pains to conceal, he jerked himself out of his chair and hurried after— on a feigned plea of politeness. Just in time to say to the Countess in a hurried, half whisper.

"If the Condesa will return, and prefer her request *alone*, it may meet with more favour."

The lady passed on, with head held dis-
dainfully, as though she heard but would not
heed. She did hear what he said, and it
brought a fresh flush upon her cheek, with
another flash of anger in her eyes. For she
could not mistake his meaning, and knew
it was as the serpent whispering into the ear
of Eve.

END OF VOL. I.

www.ingramcontent.com/pod-product-compliance
Lightning Source LLC
Chambersburg PA
CBHW030733280326
41926CB00086B/1329